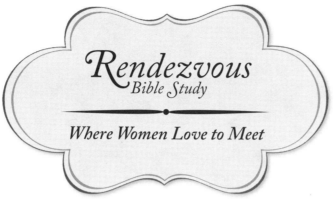

Rendezvous
Bible Study

Where Women Love to Meet

by Laura Greiner & Sharon Kohring

Joy Ride 🚲 Philippians
Bible Study Leader Guide

Group

Incredible things will happen™

Loveland, Colorado
www.group.com

Rendezvous
Joy Ride: Philippians Bible Study Leader Guide

Credits
Authors: Laura Ross Greiner and Sharon Y. Kohring
Editor/Project Manager: Amber Van Schooneveld
Senior Developer: Amy Nappa
Chief Creative Officer: Joani Schultz
Art Director: Andrea Filer
Book Designer and Cover Art Designer: Samantha Wranosky
Production Manager: DeAnne Lear

ISBN 978-0-7644-3512-6

10 9 8 7 6 5 4 3 2   16 15 14 13 12 11 10
Printed in the United States of America.

Contents

Introduction

Welcome to *Rendezvous: Joy Ride*!

We're so excited you've chosen this unique Bible study for your group. We think you'll enjoy this fresh, learner-based approach to studying the Bible. This book includes many engaging activities that will give women time to get to know one another as well as learn more about what the Bible says for living in today's crazy world. We'd like to answer some questions you may have before you begin this new adventure.

What is *Rendezvous*?

The word itself is the English form of the French word *rendez-vous*, meaning "appointment." Generally it's used as a term for gathering a group together or for setting a specific time to meet. And that's what this Bible study is all about—it's gathering women together at a specific time…but it's more than just a meeting! *Rendezvous* will create a sense of anticipation and excitement in your ministry because of two overarching goals:

- to connect women with one another in a friendly and informal setting to share their lives, grow together, and build deep and lasting relationships;

- to bring God's living Word into the daily lives of women.

So, what is *Joy Ride*?

Joy Ride is a *Rendezvous* study of the book of Philippians that offers 10 unique group sessions called "Tickets," which explore and help you discover Paul's secret to Christian joy. This short letter from Paul to the followers of Jesus in Philippi is filled with references to joy. You can count at least 14 times where the words "joy" or "rejoice" appear in the four chapters. That's pretty amazing since Paul wrote this letter while he was imprisoned in Rome. On Paul's second missionary journey, God guided him to cross over to the west, rather than staying on the eastern side of the Mediterranean. Because of that move, Philippi is home to the first church of Jesus followers in the area that we call Europe today. You can read Acts 16 and 20 to find out more about Paul's relationships and ministry in Philippi.

Field Note

Don't be discouraged if some women don't seem enthused about a certain activity. We've experienced that often those women who voice the strongest complaints before an activity are the most impacted by it.

What is the style of *Rendezvous: Joy Ride*?

Rendezvous is an interactive and experiential Bible study. Women will have many opportunities during each session for hands-on learning as well as time to share and talk through Scriptures together and think about the incredible relevance of those Scriptures for our lives today.

What is the setting for *Rendezvous: Joy Ride*?

The setting is whatever you want it to be—a small group in a home, a large group at a church, or anything in between. The material is adaptable for any size group or setting.

How much preparation time is required for *Rendezvous: Joy Ride*?

We've tried to do all of the preparatory thinking for you. You'll find in each session the following pre-teaching sections:

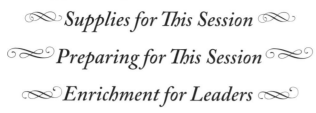

Supplies for This Session

Preparing for This Session

Enrichment for Leaders

The supplies and prep sections will let you know what you need to prepare before each session. The Enrichment for Leaders section gives you, as the leader, some encouraging thoughts to consider before the session.

In some of the sessions, there are several props and supplies to gather. We've found these hands-on activities to be helpful in women's Bible study for learning and applying Bible truths. And they also serve as an informal platform for women to get to know one another. We encourage you to adapt the activity ideas to the needs of your group. You know the best fit for your women, so don't be afraid to tweak the material for your needs and setting.

Depending on the number of women participating, we encourage you to develop a Leadership Team. Even if your team is just you and one other woman, you'll see the benefits of working alongside others. Sharing the work lightens your load and develops relationships with the women on your team. Working together creates synergy so the end results are more creative. Also, the team approach allows for weekly prayer for the *Joy Ride* women and creates a foundation of encouragement and commitment.

What if we don't have the resources to do some of the suggestions?

Don't worry if you don't have the resources for some of the activities. You can skip that activity or create your own object lesson that will work with the resources you do have. Use our suggestions to stimulate your creative thinking. Think beyond the obvious as you brainstorm! (And make it simple, too.)

How do I use the CD-ROM?

The CD-ROM included with this book contains PowerPoint slideshows to enhance your session. Slides will display verses for the women to read, questions for them to answer, and images to illustrate the message. The slides are also shown in the Leader Guide to help you follow along. As you get to the slides shown in the Leader Guide, advance to that slide during your session.

What's the Welcome Countdown Slideshow for?

The CD-ROM also includes a Welcome Countdown Slideshow to play before you start each session. It's a 1-minute slideshow of images of women set to music. We've found this to be a handy way of letting women know it's about time to start.

To Use the CD-ROM

When you place the CD-ROM in your drive, it will auto-run (it may take several seconds). If you receive a PowerPoint Viewer message with license terms, hit the accept button and the CD-ROM will auto-run.

To progress through the slides of a slideshow, use the arrow keys or your mouse's scroll button. When a slideshow is over, click on the screen, use the arrow keys, or hit escape to return to the menu. To exit a show at any time, hit escape.

There is a Rendezvous slide in between each slide of the shows for you to display while you're between slides.

PowerPoint Viewer may not be available on some Macintosh computers.

It also tells the women you are serious about starting on time, and let's them know to get ready to take their seats.

What if no one in our group is a strong speaker?

Not a problem. *Rendezvous* is specifically designed so anyone comfortable being in front of others can lead it. This isn't a Bible study that hinges on the talents of a good speaker. The material is designed to focus on the group experiences and content of the study.

To make it easy for you, suggestions for what the leader says are always highlighted in **bold print**. When you glance at any of the sessions, you'll see the bold print is interspersed and doesn't dominate the session. When there is a bold print "teaching moment," we recommend you either read it expressively or paraphrase it comfortably.

How long will each *Joy Ride* session take?

It's a good idea to allow about an hour and a half for each group session. But you can also tweak the time of the sessions according to your needs and the size of your group. Within the Leader Guide, we've given time suggestions for small group activities and interactions, but feel free to lengthen or shorten this time.

How should we set up the small groups?

The choice is yours. We've found four to six women per group is a great size. We suggest you assign groups that will stay together throughout the 10 sessions. One benefit to this approach is the relationships in the group will have an opportunity to deepen through consistent time spent together.

Another advantage with set small groups is you're able to have an "In-Touch Leader" for each group. The In-Touch Leader's role is to make a weekly point of connection with each of the women in her small group. Usually this point of connection is just a phone call or telephone message, but it can also be a cup of coffee or a lunch out together. Also, the In-Touch Leader is the person women can turn to if they have questions or concerns.

If you assign permanent small groups, allow for flexibility. Let women know they have the option of switching to another group if their small group isn't working out.

For permanent groups, you may want to consider giving each group an identity—they can create their own name and/or "look." (Or your Leadership Team could develop the options ahead of time.)

Your other option is to have women in different small groups every week. You can randomly assign them to a new group each week or have them form groups on their own each week. (We would caution you on this latter option as it allows some women to become "clique-ish.") A benefit of having different groups each week is the women get acquainted with everyone in the study and not just a select group of women.

A third option is assigning permanent groups, but once in awhile mixing it up and having women do a certain activity in a randomly assigned group.

No matter how you decide to organize your small groups, the key is flexibility and sensitivity to each woman and the overall personality of your larger group.

Who facilitates the small group?

The small group facilitation can change each week so different women have the opportunity to experience that role. You can have the small groups appoint someone new each week to facilitate that session. The role of the small group facilitator is simply to guide the group time, making sure every woman has a chance to talk.

Coffee Break

What is the Coffee Break?

For each session, we've included a "Coffee Break" section that is a short vignette based on a true, personal story that relates to the theme of that week's session. We recommend you have someone other than the leader read this story each week. It should be someone who reads well and can make the story come alive!

Another option is to have women in your group who have stories that relate to the theme of the week share their stories with the group. This works especially well for large groups, is more personal for your group, and will encourage authentic, deep relationships. If you do this, we recommend you have the woman who is going to share write her story, about three to four minutes in length, and go over it with you the week before she'll share it. This gives her time to practice and become comfortable. It also gives you the opportunity to make sure the story connects with that week's session.

Instead of choosing between the two, you could use the Coffee Break story as well as a personal story from a woman in your group. People love stories and often remember the story more than anything else.

Other recommendations to enhance your *Joy Ride*:

- ❧ Have one woman or several women take photos throughout the weeks your group is together. This will be useful for the final session.

- ❧ Read through the entire 10-week plan to get a feel for the variety in each week and to plan ahead.

- ❧ Purchase enough copies of the *Personal Guidebook for Bible Study* for each

Field Note 👉

We used different countries to identify small groups in a Bible study we led. The women really enjoyed this, and it provided some fun "international" competitions between groups.

woman to have her own. The Guidebooks are needed during each of the sessions. Small group questions and personal activities are included in the Guidebook. It's also a valuable tool to encourage women to go further in their individual relationship with God. The material in the Guidebook builds each week from the group sessions with personal enrichment ideas, thoughts for reflection, and tools for digging deeper into the Bible outside of group time. Get additional copies of the Personal Guidebook at www.group.com.

❧ Registration for the study can be very informal or more formal depending on your style and group size. You can simply have the women pay for their Guidebook, or you can provide registration forms that include information such as name, address, phone number, e-mail address, child care needs, interest in helping on the Leadership Team or being an In-Touch Leader, and so on. On the forms you can also indicate the date of registration payment. An advantage of formal registration for larger groups is it helps you know how many Guidebooks to order and how many small group In-Touch Leaders you'll need (if you pre-assign small groups). It also helps women to make a commitment to the study. Depending upon your needs, consider having a registration coordinator on your Leadership Team.

❧ Have extra Bibles available in case women forget theirs or don't have their own. You may want to make them available to purchase. For women unfamiliar with the Bible, it's helpful to provide page numbers for each session's Scriptures. (This assumes the extra Bibles you have available are all the same.) The New Living Translation of the Bible is used throughout *Rendezvous*, so try to have this version available.

❧ It's important that the women bring their Guidebook and Bible each week. Brainstorm creative ways to motivate women to succeed at this because if they forget their Guidebook, it will effect their participation in the session activities.

❧ Always open each session with a welcome to the women and with prayer. It doesn't have to be the leader who leads in prayer every time. You can have prayer led by different women each time. Or try different types of prayer, such as silent prayer, prayer in small groups, playing a worship song as prayer time, and so on.

❧ If you meet at a church, we recommend you have a hospitality person/team to create an inviting ambience each time you meet. Things to think about include chair/couch/table set up, lighting, size of the room, feel of the room (Is it cold and bare or warm and comfortable?). Also try to provide hot and cold drinks and a light snack. This provides something for early arrivers to do as they mingle and enjoy refreshments together. Greeters at the door are also helpful for larger groups.

❧ Depending on the make-up and resources of your group, you may want to provide child care or a children's ministry. Depending on the specific needs and values of your group, you may want to charge a fee for child care. If you'd like to provide children's programming during child care, visit www.group.com for great resources for kids.

❧ If your group is part of a women's ministry, you might consider having a publicity push about six weeks before you begin *Rendezvous*. For the publicity, use printed announcements in the weekly bulletins, live announcements, video clips, dramas, and so on. Again, depending on your needs, consider having a publicity coordinator on your Leadership Team.

❧ You may want to do something fun with the "ticket" idea. As mentioned above, each session of *Joy Ride* has a new theme called a "ticket." One idea is to buy a roll of tickets at your local office supply store. Hand out a ticket to the women as they arrive at each session. Make sure you know the number range of the tickets handed out. Randomly select one ticket number and award the winner with a chocolate bar, a pack of mints, a gift certificate for coffee, and so on. It can be something very small, but it's sure to add fun to your time together.

Enjoy!

We pray for you as you embark upon this *Joy Ride*! We pray specifically that each ride would show the women in your group more of what God has for all of us—a life infused with his joy!

With joy,

Laura and Sharon

A Thankful Heart Is a Joyful Heart

⊷ Supplies for This Session ⊷

☞ green, blue, and purple very thin, silky ribbon cut in 8-inch strips, enough so each woman has a strand of each color

☞ small pieces of scrap paper, enough so each woman has three pieces

☞ pens

☞ *VeggieTales: Madame Blueberry* DVD (available from the library, bookstore, the Internet, or from your church's video library)

☞ one brown lunch bag

⊷ Preparing for This Session ⊷

Cut the ribbon into 8-inch strips and put the ribbons, grouped by color, on a table. Obtain a copy of the *VeggieTales: Madame Blueberry* DVD and preview it before the session. Cue it to the "I'm So Blue" song, about five minutes into the video. If possible, arrange for blueberries to be in all snacks provided for this session (blueberry coffee cake, blueberry scones, blueberry muffins, blueberry cobbler, and so on). Before the session, tie the three different colored ribbons to your wrist.

⊷ Enrichment for Leaders ⊷

This session reminds us that a thankful heart is an important piece of our Joy Ride with God. If you have time, pick up the book *Radical Gratitude: Discovering Joy Through Everyday Thankfulness* by Ellen Vaughn and read it before this session.

1. *Thanksgiving All Year Round*

Point to the slide.

Say: **What would that look like—to have the Thanksgiving spirit all year round?**

Have women form small groups and let them talk about the two questions on the slide. After five to ten minutes, come back as a larger group and have one person from each of the smaller groups share a couple favorite traditions and ways we could have the Thanksgiving spirit more throughout the year.

Slide 1.1

2. *Thankfulness*

Say: **There are two verses in Philippians we'll chew on during our time together that will help us think about being thankful in our everyday lives.**

Read or ask a volunteer to read the verses on the slide. Then have women write the verses down in their Personal Guidebooks on page 5 so they can refer to them throughout today's study.

Helpful Hint ☞

If you have a large group of women, have one person per table get the ribbons for her table, or place the ribbons on each table in advance.

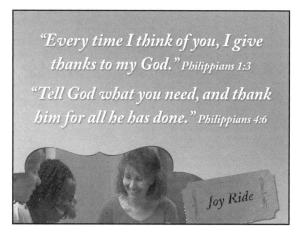

Slide 1.2

Have women get the three different ribbons from the table. (They need one of each color.)

Say: These are our reminder ribbons. They're going to remind us of three different aspects Paul shows us about being thanks-givers.

• *The blue ribbon is our "First-Thing Ribbon."*

Ask the women to help each other tie this ribbon around their wrists.

Ask the women to close their eyes and picture someone they love who doesn't live close by. Keeping their eyes closed, have them continue thinking about that person. Wait for about 30 seconds. Ask them to open their eyes and write down in their Guidebook who they pictured and the first thing they thought of when they pictured that person.

Give the women a minute to write down their responses.

Say: The first thing that comes to Paul's mind when he thinks about his beloved friends in Philippi is how thankful he is for them.

Reread Philippians 1:3:

"Every time I think of you, I give thanks to my God." Paul shows us in this verse that one aspect of being a good thanks-giver is to first thank God. Our blue ribbon is a reminder to first and foremost thank God.

(Hold up your wrist with a blue ribbon on it.)

Thanking God needs to come to the top of our list when we pray.

• *The green ribbon is our "Every-Time Ribbon."*

Have the women help each other tie on the green ribbon.

Paul also shows us how being thanks-givers is not a one-Thursday- in-November arrangement with God. It's an everyday, "every-time" piece of our prayer life.

Reread Philippians 1:3.

When we reread this verse, we see thanksgiving is the first thing Paul does and he does it every time. He shows us not only that it is a priority but a *repetitive necessity*.

Give an example of this. You can use the example below or come up with your own.

> *The need to continually repeat our thanks to God is kind of like reminding your child to say thank you to a carpool mom every time he or she is driven to school. You don't tell your child to say "thanks" once at the beginning of the year. "Thanks Mrs. Jones for giving me a ride to school every Tuesday and Thursday this year." No, you teach him or her to say thanks every time they're given a ride.*

Helpful Hint ☞
It's helpful to have a noisemaker, such as a bell, to get everyone's attention after small group time or writing time. The sound is a less intrusive way to transition into the next section. Visit www.group.com for noisemaker ideas.

Paul shows us it's the same for us with God. We need to *say thanks anew each day.*

• *The purple ribbon is our "All Ribbon."*

Have the women help each other tie on the purple ribbon.

Reread Philippians 4:6:

"Tell God what you need, and thank him for all he has done." Paul is telling us here that every time we go to God with our needs we are to take time to thank him for *all* he has done.

Pass out small pieces of paper and pens so each woman has three pieces. Ask the women to write down three prayer needs they have right now so each piece of paper has one need. Let the women know these prayer needs will be mixed together then read out loud.

If necessary, give examples of prayer needs, such as "for our finances," "for my son to make new friends," or "for my husband to find a job."

Say: **Paul shows us a two-part formula: Tell God what we need + thank Him for all he has done. We're going to take the needs we've written down and practice this formula.**

Have the women fold their pieces of paper and collect the folded pieces of paper in a brown lunch bag. (Let women know they won't need to "own-up" to the prayers they wrote down. This is just an exercise to get them practicing Paul's formula.)

Hand the brown bag to a woman in the group, and ask her to pull out one piece of paper and read it. Then practice together what it would look like using Paul's formula. Have different women pull prayer needs from the bag and practice together for about five to 10 minutes.

> *Helpful Hint* 👉
>
> If you have a large group of women, place the pens and pieces of paper at each chair or table before the meeting to save time.

Example of Practicing Paul's Formula:

Sample prayer need: *"For our finances and my husband's unemployment. We're really struggling this month."*

Practice the formula: *Pray for the need + thank God for what he has done.*

• *"Help us, Lord, to pay our bills this month + thank you, God, for your faithfulness in the past."*

• *"Help me sleep better and not to worry so much + thank you for caring about my every need."*

• *"I pray for my husband's interview tomorrow. I pray this job is a good fit for him and that he's offered the job + thank you for the job contacts you've given so far."*

Say: The formula is very simple. We all need to get better at thinking about how we can thank God when we pray for our needs. The bottom line is: We need to think about thanking more!

(Hold up your wrist with the three ribbons.)

Now that we have our three ribbons that remind us of some key ingredients in thankfulness, how do we get there? Let's learn some lessons from Madame Blueberry.

3. Lessons From Madame Blueberry

Show the beginning segment of *VeggieTales: Madame Blueberry*, where Madame Blueberry sings the "I'm So Blue" song (about five minutes into it). Play until the end of the song. If you'd like, have women nibble on blueberry snacks as they watch!

After the clip, explain how Madame Blueberry tried in vain to find fulfillment in her life through buying more stuff. But it's a thankful heart that yields happiness—not stuff!

Have volunteers read the following short vignettes (or read them yourself).

Amy

Amy always compared herself to others. She envied her best friend, Jillian, the most. Jillian had a seemingly perfect figure and an amazing wardrobe to go with it. To deal with her envy, Amy would spend money she didn't have on clothes she didn't need. Shopping always made her feel so much better. Her mood was always lifted when she came home with a great new outfit. But the exhilaration was short lived, and the need for another, cuter outfit came whenever she had a bad day or was feeling bad about herself.

Sandy

Sandy married a guy who didn't have a lot of money and whose line of work would never make them wealthy. It was hard for Sandy to watch her friends' husbands making a lot of money. When one of her friends, Dawn, bought a huge, beautiful home, Sandy could hardly stand it. She coveted the home with its wrap-around porch and enormous state-of-the-art kitchen. Her feelings of jealousy strained her friendship with Dawn. It also wreaked havoc in her marriage because she continually

made comments to her husband about how little they had compared to all of her friends.

Bella

Something inside Bella's heart felt empty and unsatisfied. She couldn't put her finger on it, she just wanted more. But she wasn't sure what she wanted more of. She had a good job; she had three healthy kids and a doting husband. Why was she so unsatisfied? Her dissatisfaction made her depressed. She knew there had to be more to life, but what? Where? She searched for an answer. Maybe if she exercised and got in really good shape she would feel better about things. Maybe if she and her husband took exciting trips she would feel more fulfilled. Maybe if she pursued another degree she would have more satisfaction. Her search led her down many empty trails, and each time she was left feeling like something was still missing.

Slide 1.3

Say: **Think about these different women. How can you relate to them? Shop to drown out your blues? Covet your neighbors stuff? Unsatisfied with what you have?**

Have women return to their small groups and discuss the "More, More, More" Nudge Questions on page 6 of their Guidebooks. Allow five to 10 minutes for their discussion.

When we're unsatisfied with what we have, looking for something else or coveting more, we can't be thankful.

Ask for a volunteer to come stand next to you. When she's standing there, ask

Helpful Hint ☞

It's always good for the group to pick one person during the Nudge questions to ask the questions and make sure everyone has a turn sharing.

her to stay standing next to you and also go stand at the back of the room. (Of course she won't be able to do it.)

You can't stand in two places at the same time, right? It's the same with being a thanks-giver. You can't be like Madame Blueberry and be a thanks-giver.

4. *Practice*

It takes intentional practice to become a good thanks-giver. Listen to how one woman practiced.

Read the following story.

> *I was very in love with my husband, but he fell in love with a younger woman and moved out. He stopped supporting me and our two children, and I had to go back to work. I loved staying at home with my kids, but now I work over 50 hours a week and seem to miss out on so much. Sometimes I feel myself stuck in the miry pit of my life. One thing that helps me get out of the pit is to think about all I do have. Every morning as I drive into work, I make myself tell the Lord everything I'm thankful for.* I'm thankful I have a good job so I can provide for my kids. I'm thankful for the great friends and the support I have. I'm thankful my kids are doing really well in school and that I have a very close relationship with them. I'm thankful for the great school they are in and all the friends they have. *I just keep going down the list and focus on everything I have to be thankful for. By the time I get to work my heart is full and I actually feel really thankful.*

Ask one of the women to read out loud the "A-Z Thanks-Giver Ideas" on page 6 of the Guidebook.

On page 8 of their Guidebooks, have women trace one of their hands. Tell the women to write down five ideas in the five fingers they would like to practice. They can use the ideas from the "A-Z Thanks-Giver Ideas" list or they can come up with their own.

5. *Why Should We Become Better Thanks-Givers?*

***Say:* We've covered how to be a good thanks-giver with our blue, green, and purple ribbons. We've covered when and where through our**

brainstorming and practicing. Now let's look at why we should become good thanks-givers.

One simple reason is because we want to experience the Joy Ride like Paul. There he was in prison. He'd lost his freedom, he was eating prison food, he was desperately lonely for his friends, and yet he was brimming with joy. Why so much joy in the midst of his hardly ideal circumstances? A big piece of the reason is because he was a very good thanks-giver. Let's hear more about this from a woman's perspective.

Before this session, ask a woman from your group to share a story from her life about a time she learned to thank God at all times. If there's not a woman from your group who can share, have a volunteer read the following story. Have this volunteer practice before the session so she can read with passion!

Renee

A shift took place inside me about a year ago after I heard a woman at our church teach on having an "attitude of gratitude." Before that point, I never thought too much about being thankful. I mean I did the basics: I taught my kids to be thankful, I thanked God before a meal, and most of the times when God answered a specific prayer, I remembered to thank him. But truthfully, walking around with an "attitude of gratitude" wasn't a priority for me. Life was too busy. There were so many people around me facing really hard things like a struggling marriage or illness that focusing on thanksgiving wasn't something I did much.

But this changed for me after a guest speaker came to a Wednesday morning Bible study I was in. She taught on thankfulness. She told the story from Luke 17:11-19 about the 10 lepers whom Jesus healed and how only one out of the 10 came back to thank Jesus for healing him. As she told the story, my stomach tightened. I wanted to be the one that

came back and said thank you, but I knew I wasn't. I was in the group of nine who got too involved in the moment to stop, go back, and say thank you. Ugh! I hated that realization about myself.

The woman gave suggestions on how to get in the habit of being thankful. I took notes as she talked. One thing she suggested was to set the alarm on your watch and have it go off at a certain time each day. When the alarm goes off, she said it was a good reminder to take a few minutes and spend time just thanking God. I can't even change the time on my watch every year when it's daylight-saving time, so the technical challenge of that suggestion was too much for me, and I didn't even write it down.

That evening, I was at home helping my kids with their homework. My 5-year-old son started pushing the buttons on my watch to make the light go on. I let him fool around with it for a while and then sent him off to get ready for bed. The next day at noon, the alarm on my watch went off. Not thinking much about it, I pushed at the different buttons and found one that made the beeping stop. It went off again the next day at noon. On the third day, I was sitting in front of my computer working. I remembered Sammy playing with my watch and guessed he had inadvertently set my alarm to go off every day at noon. I also remembered the woman's suggestion at Bible study. But I was in the middle of typing up a report, and I only had another hour to get it done. The last thing I wanted to do was stop, even for a minute, and give thanks. I tried to ignore the nagging feeling in my heart and kept working. Finally, the nag grew too loud, and I stopped typing. I closed my eyes. *Thank you, God, for all of this work in front of me. Thank you that you are with me. Thank you for helping me get it done. Thank you for this reminder to stop and just give you thanks.* I kept thanking God for another minute or so and then began to work again.

For more than a year now, thanks to whatever Sammy did to my watch, the alarm goes off every day at 12 noon. And I've learned to stop what I'm doing and give thanks. It's such a small thing, but it has made a difference. This little habit has snuck into my life like a stick of dynamite—igniting in me a spirit of thankfulness I never had before.

I find myself thanking God all of the time now, and not just when the alarm starts to beep.

I think thankfulness is like the yeast in bread that Jesus talked about. He said a little bit of yeast permeates every part of a piece of dough. That one little pause in my day has permeated my spiritual life like a refreshing breeze. And in this journey of learning how to be more thankful, I've found that my heart is lighter. I've found my spirit feels fuller. I have found more joy.

And I'm thankful!

6. *Wrap It Up*

To remember the significance of their ribbons, have the women look at the slide and write down in their Guidebooks on page 8 what each ribbon represents. Tell them that at the end of the day when they take off their ribbons, they can place them in their Guidebooks as a reminder to be thankful.

Slide 1.4

Say: The woman in the story we just heard, like Madame Blueberry, learned that a thankful heart yields a joyful heart.

Here's a challenge for you for this week: Do one thing you wrote on your hand to practice being a thanks-giver this week and come back and share it with your group next week. Write it in your Guidebook on the handprint, so you don't forget!

Before the women head out, close your time together in prayer.

Joy, Certainly!

❧ Supplies for This Session ❧

- ☞ *Sound of Music* DVD
- ☞ 3 chairs: one that is obviously broken, one that is unstable but not noticeably broken, one that is solid
- ☞ all-day lipcolor such as Outlast by Covergirl (preferably a bright color) and a regular tinted lip gloss such as Smoothwear Liptints by Covergirl
- ☞ costume for "Paul" (a striped head "scarf" with a band, a robe-like "gown," a tasseled belt, brown sandals, long dark-haired wig)
- ☞ volunteer to wear the Paul costume and do a dramatic reading of 2 Corinthians 11:17-29

❧ Preparing for This Session ❧

Cue the *Sound of Music* DVD to the correct spot (about 18 minutes into the movie) so it's ready to play. Have the three chairs set up in front before you begin this session.

❧ Enrichment for Leaders ❧

Ever feel like the "little engine that couldn't"? Sometimes "I think I can" just isn't enough. So what do we do when we're out of self-confidence? As you prepare for this session, consider how our joy is stabilized by God-confidence. Every time you ask God for help this week, picture him gently saying to you, "You can't do this thing, but I can!"

1. Let's Take a Look

Begin this session in small groups of four to six. After welcoming the women, encourage them to share ways they were able to demonstrate a thankful heart in the past week and how their efforts yielded joy.

Slide 2.1

Allow about five minutes. While they're still in small groups, lead women in a prayer of thankfulness for your time together today. Then have the women reconvene as a large group.

On the *Sound of Music* DVD, play the scene when Maria sings the "I Have Confidence" song (about 18 minutes into the film). End the clip after Maria sings the last few verses, looks through the gate, and says, "Oh, help!" (You want to end the song right after she says this and before she continues to the end.)

Say: **What is confidence? Before we define what it is, let's look at what it isn't.**

Ask the women to share in their small groups behaviors that might look like they reflect confidence but really are *not*. Examples are cockiness, arrogance, or being in denial. After a few minutes, have several groups report back their thoughts. Discuss why these things aren't the same as confidence.

Using the three pre-arranged chairs, ask for three volunteers to sit in each of the chairs. Don't assign any woman to any particular chair. Allow them to work it out. Allow several minutes for them to try the chairs and respond. Then have them return to their regular seats.

Discuss what the audience observed and experienced. Ask:

• **Did some of the chair-sitters doubt? Did some have misplaced confidence?**

• **How did we feel watching? Worried? Wanting to advise?**

• **Did anyone have a good reason to be confident?**

• **How did each one's level of confidence change during the experience?**

• How did the audience affect the confidence of the participants?

2. Confidence Understood

Say: There are two components of confidence. The first is the holder of the confidence, and the second is the object in which the confidence is placed.

Which of these is the most important component? Why?

(Answers may vary.)

Point to the unstable chair.

When I sit down in this chair, I might be very confident that it will hold me. But if the chair is unstable, my confidence doesn't mean much. Right?

Have someone read Philippians 1:6.

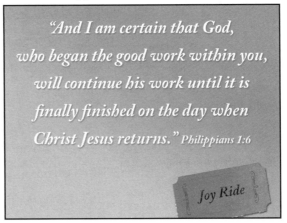

"And I am certain that God, who began the good work within you, will continue his work until it is finally finished on the day when Christ Jesus returns." Philippians 1:6

Joy Ride

Slide 2.2

Have the women take a minute to read in their Guidebook on page 13 about the word "certain."

The original Greek word used for "certain" in this verse carried the idea of being persuaded, as in "I didn't always feel this way but now, because of _____ [some event], I am now persuaded. I am now convinced. I have no doubt."

Reread Philippians 1:6.

Say: **Paul made a very confident statement when he said, "I am *certain* that God…*will* continue his work until it is finally finished." Is this statement more about the holder of the confidence or more about the object in which the confidence is placed?**

Allow the women time to reflect and respond. (His confidence was not in himself or in others. His confidence was solely in the fact that God is able.

God began the good work in them, so Paul was *certain* that God would carry it through.) Then introduce the woman sharing her story, or the reader who will share about confidence from a woman's perspective.

Coffee Break

Before this session, ask a woman from your group to share a story from her life about a time she learned to find confidence in God, not herself. If there's not a woman from your group who can share, have a volunteer read the following story. Have this volunteer practice before the session so she can read with passion!

Jillian

I wanted to be a good wife, really I did. But the truth was I stunk. Jordan and I got married young, and we were bullheaded, immature, and self-centered ignoramuses. (Pardon the vernacular, but it is the only word to really describe us.) We fought more than any other couple I knew, and, get this, we were youth group leaders at our church. I can't count how many times we would get into a huge fight then have to lead a Bible study together. It was awful. My biggest problem was my volatile mouth. I was like a pack of firecrackers, and my mouth was where the explosives went off.

I tried and tried to control my tongue and be a better wife, but things didn't get better. The intense fighting continued. I remember one time after a big fight Jordan stormed out of our apartment, and I sat curled up on the family room couch. It had gotten dark, but I hadn't bothered to turn on any lights. I was too discouraged to move and just sat there crying and vowing I would change. *I'm not going to say anything anymore. I am going to keep my mouth shut*, I declared to the dark room. But, somehow that declaration didn't feel like enough. I needed more. In childish desperation, I got up and grabbed a Bible from the side table at

the other end of the couch. Putting my hand on top of it I vowed: *Next time we get into an argument, I will hold my tongue. I will be patient and have self control. I will remain calm and composed. I will not open my mouth.*

It was only a few weeks later when I engaged in more verbal combat with Jordan, my vow being thrown out the front door. No matter how hard I tried, I couldn't seem to change myself.

God showed me over the next several years how my self-determination wasn't what I needed. The change inside me began one fall when I signed up for a women's Bible study. I had led and participated in many Bible studies in the past, but my heart was at a different place this time. I was broken and weary and ready for more of God. During that particular study, I hungered for God in a way I'd never experienced before. I no longer wanted to just follow Christ. I wanted to run after him. I began getting up every morning at 5:00 a.m. and reading my Bible. The weird thing was it wasn't a chore or a duty. It was my favorite part of the day. I learned that what I needed was God to change me, to do a work inside me, because of who *he* is. I needed to draw close to him because he does the changing.

I've been married to Jordan 25 years now, and I am a different wife, a different person. I'm not perfect, of course, but once I shifted my confidence over from myself to God, I saw first hand how he had a mighty work to do in my life. I know through a lot of failed attempts that placing confidence in myself is ineffective and unstable. It's only God's work inside us that's lasting and dependable.

Everyday I tell him I want him to finish what he has begun inside me. I want to become everything he has set out for me to be!

3. Confidence Shifted

Say: **We each need to make that switch from confidence in ourselves to confidence in God. Paul was always a bold man, but something within him changed at one point in his life. He moved from self-confidence to God-confidence!**

Ask the women to form their small groups and read Acts 9:1-21 together, which is printed in their Guidebooks on page 13. Have them discuss and write down in their Guidebooks a few key points of the Saul-to-Paul story.

Then ask the groups to discuss:

Why was Paul so bold about God's abilities and faithfulness?

(This question is printed in their Guidebooks on page 15.) Have each small group share with the larger group some of the things they discussed.

Conclude:

Saul was a very self-confident man, but when he encountered God and experienced his power personally, his confidence moved from himself to God.

4. Confidence Lived

Read Philippians 3:3.

Paul relied on what Jesus had done for him, which he knew was lasting and enduring.

"For we who worship by the Spirit of God are the ones who are truly circumcised. We rely on what Christ Jesus has done for us. We put no confidence in human effort."
Philippians 3:3

Slide 2.3

Ask for two volunteers. Have them come up front. Hold up the all-day lipstick and the lip gloss. Have one of the volunteers apply the all-day lipstick and the other volunteer apply the lip gloss. Explain how the all-day lipstick will last up to 16 hours, while the regular lip gloss may last less than a half an hour before it fades. Have the volunteers "model" their lipstick with different poses such as a pucker, a pout, and a smile.

Explain that Paul was putting on, choosing something, that he knew was lasting and enduring—like the all-day lipstick. Whereas confidence in ourselves is more like the tinted lip gloss—short-lived and needing to be reapplied—the power of confidence in God is lasting.

Let your volunteers know they can have a seat and you'll call them back up in a little bit to check and see how their lip color is holding up.

Say: **Paul didn't rely on himself although he had plenty of human reasons he could have.**

Helpful Hint

Include everyone! Ask each woman to look in her purse for lipstick, lip gloss, or even lip balm, and put some on. Later on, they can compare with their neighbors how theirs is holding up. This let's everyone be a participant.

Read Philippians 3:4-6.

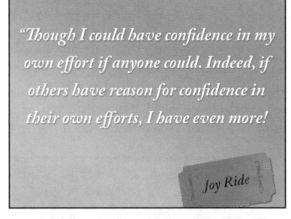

"Though I could have confidence in my own effort if anyone could. Indeed, if others have reason for confidence in their own efforts, I have even more!

Joy Ride

Slide 2.4

...I was circumcised when I was eight days old. I am a pure-blooded citizen of Israel and a member of the tribe of Benjamin—a real Hebrew if there ever was one! I was a member of the Pharisees,

Joy Ride

Slide 2.5

...who demand the strictest obedience to the Jewish law. I was so zealous that I harshly persecuted the church. And as far as righteousness, I obeyed the law without fault." Philippians 3:4-6

Joy Ride

Slide 2.6

So if anyone could be confident, it was Paul. He had all the credentials.

Have the lights go dark, and have your reader dressed as Paul sneak up to the front. If possible, put a bright spotlight on her. Otherwise, bring all lights back up.

Dramatic Reading: "Paul" Reads 2 Corinthians 11:17-29

"Such boasting is not from the Lord, but I am acting like a fool. And since others boast about their human achievements, I will, too. After all, you think you are so wise, but you enjoy putting up with fools! You put up with it when someone enslaves you, takes everything you have, takes advantage of you, takes control of everything, and slaps you in the face. I'm ashamed to say that we've been too "weak" to do that!

But whatever they dare to boast about—I'm talking like a fool again—I dare to boast about it, too. Are they Hebrews? So am I. Are they Israelites? So am I. Are they descendants of Abraham? So am I. Are they servants of Christ? I know I sound like a madman, but I have served him far more! I have worked harder, been put in prison more often, been whipped times without number, and faced death again and again. Five different times the Jewish leaders gave me thirty-nine lashes. Three times I was beaten with rods. Once I was stoned. Three times I was shipwrecked. Once I spent a whole night and a day adrift at sea. I have traveled on many long journeys. I have faced danger from rivers and from robbers. I have faced danger from my own people, the Jews, as well as from the Gentiles. I have faced danger in the cities, in the deserts, and on the seas. And I have faced danger from men who claim to be believers but are not. I have worked hard and long, enduring many sleepless nights. I have been hungry and thirsty and have often gone without food. I have shivered in the cold, without enough clothing to keep me warm.

Then, besides all this, I have the daily burden of my concern for all the churches. Who is weak without my feeling that weakness? Who is led astray and I do not burn with anger?"

Have your reader take a bow and have a seat. Then ask:

What was Paul saying, really? Why was he talking like he was boasting?

(He wanted to show them if anyone got into a boasting contest with him, he'd win. But that's not what mattered. He had learned that confidence in himself wasn't what mattered. What mattered was confidence in Christ!)

Call up your lipstick volunteers, and have the group take a look at how the lipsticks are lasting. Have a little fun with this, asking the volunteers to pucker up and kiss a piece of blank white paper. Then check their lips again.

Ask the audience which lipstick is more enduring. Hold up the two lipsticks and reiterate that the one is like Christ confidence, enduring, and the other is like self-confidence, fading.

Thank the volunteers with a round of applause.

5. Confidence Embraced

Say: **We all have faith in something. Think about it. Even those who claim to have no faith and say, "no one can really know the truth," are putting their faith in the truth of their statement. We all have faith in something. The question is not "do you have confidence?" but "where do you place your confidence?"**

Have women write in their Guidebooks one thing in which they've placed their confidence that has failed them.

Have women get into their small groups. Have them share a time when they misplaced confidence in something that didn't last and learned the hard way that their certainty was in the wrong place. (Assure them it doesn't have to be what they wrote in their Guidebook. It could be a "safer" example.)

Slide 2.7

Say: **When you climb into a canoe, what direction do you face? Forward. If you're alone, you grab one paddle and you control where you go from the back of the canoe with fancy "J" strokes. If you're good, the canoe won't wobble back and forth. If you're really good, it might glide for a while. But in a canoe, you always anticipate a snag, an obstacle like a big rock or the fast water that's ahead of you. You must look ahead and never lose control.**

Say: **When you climb into a rowboat, what direction do you face? Backward. If you're alone, you grab both oars and focus on a point that is stable on the shore. You move where you need to go while you face backward and confidently row that boat. If we can do this, we become more confident women. In a rowboat, you pick a place on the shore to focus on that helps you stay oriented as you steer the boat. In life we need to focus on God; it is he who will help us confidently forge ahead.**

Slide 2.8

Still in their small groups, have the women discuss the "Confidence" Nudge Questions in their Guidebooks on page 15. After about 10 minutes, invite

the women to pray together in their groups, focusing their prayer on areas where they struggle with putting confidence in something other than God. Let them know when they hear the soft music, it's time to wrap up their prayer and reconvene as a large group.

After five to 10 minutes, play music to encourage the groups to return to the large group.

6. Wrap It Up

Say: **God is calling each of us to climb into his rowboat every day of our lives. We don't exactly know where we're going. We don't know how we'll get there. We can't anticipate what is ahead. But we can grab both oars and start moving with confidence** *because we are focused on God's stable, faithful goodness to us in the past.* **We can say, "I can trust God with my future because he has been faithful in my past."**

Under the rowboat in their Guidebooks on page 16, have women write a commitment to climb into God's rowboat and put their confidence in God. They could write a prayer, write down a verse that they want to remember, or write a goal.

We can have the joy God has for us because we're not left to handle life on our own. We're in God's boat, and we can rejoice in the *certain* **knowledge that God is protecting us and guiding us. When we ask ourselves, "Can I have joy in this circumstance?" our answer is "***certainly!***"**

Close with prayer:

Thank you, Father, for your patience with us even though so often we have more self-confidence than God-confidence. Give us the strength to climb into your rowboat everyday. Help us this week to consciously choose to put our confidence in you and not in the things and people around us. Thank you for the joy that comes from that kind of stability!

Joyfully Ever After

❧ Supplies for This Session ❧

☞ lollipops, enough for one small group (if your small groups are six women, have six lollipops)

☞ adding machine paper, cut into 2-foot lengths, enough for one piece for each small group

☞ pens

❧ Preparing for This Session ❧

Practice the "viewfinder" activity on page 31 until you can do it easily yourself.

❧ Enrichment for Leaders ❧

Consider this—God, the omnipotent creator of the universe, the risen Lord who suffered to redeem our lives from the mess of sin, the Holy Spirit who is residing within us—*He* is not baffled or bewildered by anything that happens in our days. We're the ones who are shocked. We're small; he's big. We're clueless; he's clued in. It's really that simple. If we look at our life from God's perspective—wow, things would look very different. As you prepare this week, ask God to give you the ability to see the world more through his eyes each day! Pray for an eternal rather than an earthly perspective.

1. Ready for a Change

Have women form small groups as they arrive. Give each small group a pen and a piece of adding machine paper that is 2 feet long. Tell them not to begin until you say "go!" Tell them that they will be racing to write the longest and most valid list of things in our lives that will matter for eternity. Ask for clarifying questions. Give the groups no more than five minutes to finish.

After five minutes, have one representative from each group bring their list to the front and read it. Audience members can challenge the validity of anything listed. The leader (or some other designated "judge") has veto or acceptance power. After every group has read its list, reward the representative of the group with the longest and most valid list lollipops for her group.

Slide 3.1

Say: Close your eyes. Imagine God in heaven looking down on all of us, looking specifically at a crisis in your life and wringing his hands in bewilderment saying, "I didn't know it was going to go this way. Now what do I do? Oh, what do I do?"

Open your eyes. A pathetic image, right? Laughable, even! But very close to reality! "What?" you say, "I never think God does that." Well, we live like we believe it! Often, when we are in a crisis, we bring God down to our level, and in our mind we treat God, the omnipotent creator of the universe, like an impotent little human!

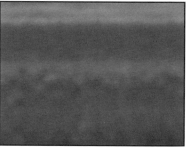

Slide 3.2

Move through each slide, 1 through 4, without speaking, allowing time for women's eyes to struggle to focus.

Say: Isn't it amazing how different life can seem if we change our view?

Have women stand up and hold their arms out straight in front of them, elbows locked, wrists bent back, palms out. Overlap hands but leave a space for a "viewfinder" between your thumbs and the rest of your fingers.

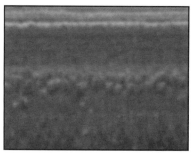

Slide 3.3

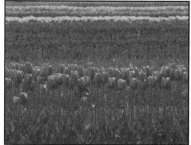

Slide 3.4

Ask the women to pick an object to stare at through their "viewfinder" with both eyes. Tell them to keep their hands still and close their left eye. Then, have them keep their hands still and open their left eye and close their right eye. (The object will disappear from view when their dominant eye is closed and they're using their weaker eye.)

Something changes! What changed?

Have the women briefly discuss what changed with a partner. They can try the viewfinder exercise a couple more times and test the change.

2. Leaving the Dark Side

Say: **The filter we see through colors our world and can be a joy-booster or a joy-buster. Even if two people are looking at the same thing, what they see varies if they look at it from a different internal view.**

Slide 3.5

Have a volunteer read the short story below while Slide 5 is projected on the screen. Before the reading ask:

What's your internal view? Listen to this story, and see which person's view is more like yours.

> *Two people are in the same car, taking in the same things as they drive down the Alaskan highway. Person A is in awe of the mountains that stretch skyward from the sea; she peers at the massive river as they cross over a bridge, and the glacier takes her breath away as it seems just beyond reach of the river's edge. Person B says, "Man, you don't have any billboards to read during this drive. That makes this drive so long. I don't know how you do it. Booooooring!"*

Say: **If we use a narrow filter like Person B, what we see will be limited— negating any joy God might have for us in that moment. But if we see from a wider filter with a more eternal picture, we're bound to be boosted and uplifted just like Person A who was struck and inspired by the beauty all around her—the same beauty that Person B had also seen but missed.**

Have someone read Philippians 3:18-19.

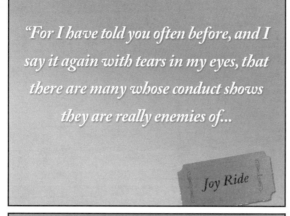

Slide 3.6

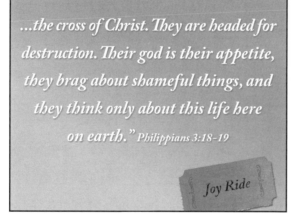

Slide 3.7

Say: **For those on the dark side, Paul says that their destiny is destruction. What is it they do that will lead to destruction?**

(They think only about this life here on earth.)

Oops. That sounds like…well, it sounds like me on most days. Does it sound like you? Often because our feet are firmly planted on earth, our minds are often there, too.

Paul had lived from that place, too. Feet and mind firmly planted on earth. But that changed because of Jesus.

Have the group read together Philippians 3:7-8.

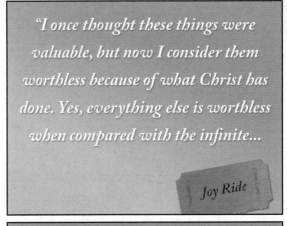

Slide 3.8

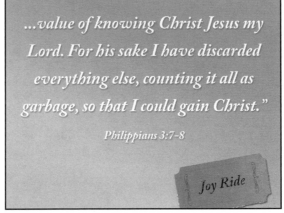

Slide 3.9

Say: Those things in his life that had once been in the plus column ("valuable, to my profit") were now in the loss column ("loss, rubbish, worthless").

Instruct the women to write in their Guidebooks on page 21 some things in the "Once Considered Valuable" column things that they used to place a lot of stock in. Then in the "Now Considered Not Worth Much" column, have them write what they now find valueless. For example, they might write in the "Once Considered Valuable" column "owning a big home," and in the "Now Considered Not Worth Much" column "gaining material things." (Allow about four minutes for this.) Then, instruct the women to turn to a neighbor and share some things they wrote down. (Allow a few minutes for this.)

After the time of sharing, let women know it's time to hear from a woman who has gone through this struggle herself.

Coffee Break

Before this session, ask a woman from your group to share a story from her life about a time she learned that what she was considering gain was really worthless and her joy came from someplace else. If there's not a woman from your group who can share, have a volunteer read the following story. Have this volunteer practice before the session so she can read with passion!

Jolette

Right now there aren't a lot of reasons for me to "feel" joyful. I'll net it out for you. I've been separated from my husband, Darren, three different times during our 13 years of marriage, largely because of his infidelity and verbal abuse. This most recent separation looks like the end. I drew boundaries about things I could no longer live with, and he went berserk, blaming me for his unfaithfulness and verbal rage. He has started the paperwork for divorce, and it looks like only a matter of time until we're officially over.

It would seem like this is a good thing based on how horrible he treats me, but the reality is…I hate divorce. My parents got divorced when I was young, and I vowed I would never put my kids through that. Now, my 12-year-old daughter and 8-year-old son are about to be split between Darren and me permanently. And that kills me. Another big reason I've hung onto this marriage is because my whole life, all I've ever wanted is to be a stay-at-home mom with a wonderful family. Weekly my son says to me, "Mommy I wish we could all be together." Whenever he colors a picture, it's always of the four of us. I think if you took a knife and jabbed it into my heart, it would hurt less.

But here's the really unbelievable thing—I have a deep sense of joy even as my dreams crumble around me. I had a friend tell me just this past weekend that I was more joyful than some of the "happily" married women she knew. She said the joy of the Lord is all over my face. I don't know about my face, but I know his joy is in my heart. And it comes from hope I find when I read the Bible. I've found that I have to stay in the Bible, reading it in the morning and before I go to bed at night. Otherwise I start to sink into the depressing reality of my life. If I'm not doing so well, I turn to the Psalms and always find comfort. Those times when I haven't been committed to reading God's word, the joy inside me subsides and I become overwhelmed and immensely sad.

Another reason for my joy is what I think about. I think a lot about how I'm just passing through this life. I know this life is a blink of an eye. The pain and sadness of my broken marriage is *not* permanent. God promises he will make all things new in heaven. I don't know exactly what this looks like, but I do know the heartache in my life right now is temporary and I have an eternity of wholeness ahead of me. When I think of life in terms of his big picture, it's like a makeover on my insides. It always renews my weary spirit and gives me hope for the future. It also gives me a determination to do my life well today.

In spite of everything we've been through, I desperately want our marriage to work. But my marriage and Darren's decisions don't dictate my life or my joy. It surprises me to hear myself saying this in the middle of a divorce because it's so irrational. But it's true. As long as I stay focused on the eternal hope of Christ, I know his joy. It pours into me in spite of everything else.

3. Reality Check

> *Say:* **We have two realities:**
>
> **1. Our physical lives here on earth, the things we see.**
>
> **2. Our spiritual lives, which last for eternity. We are eternal beings now!**
>
> **It's like two sides of a coin. Both are real but in this case, only one side lasts forever!**

Have women turn to the illustration of the coins in their Guidebook on page 22. Instruct them to write next to one side of the coin things in their own life that will not last for eternity (house address, hair color, weight, and so on). Next to the other side of the coin, have them write down things they've done over the past two months that matter for eternity (attending a Bible study,

giving money to someone in need, visiting someone who is lonely, praying, encouraging, and so on). Allow up to five minutes for this.

Have women move into their small groups and share their coins with the group, allowing five to 10 minutes for sharing. Have them discuss the "Ever After" Nudge Questions in their Guidebooks on page 22. After about 10-15 minutes of discussion, ask them to return to the large group.

4. Wrap It Up

Say: **What's more real? The stuff you can touch but can vanish into thin air at any moment or the stuff that lasts forever?**

Your passport is not from this earth, but heaven. And when we walk through life with a heaven-oriented perspective, we're open to receive more of God's joy.

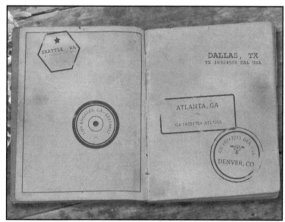

Slide 3.10

In this next week, spend at least five minutes each night before you go to sleep reviewing the spiritual realities of your day: the things that touched your life or that you did that will last for eternity. Record those things in your Guidebook on the Rendezvous for Two page.

Let's close in prayer. God, thank you so much that you have joy for us each and every day. Help us not to see our lives from our earthly perspective, but from your heavenly, eternal perspective. Affirm in our hearts that we can have joy happily ever after because our eternal home is with you.

Multiply the Joy!

❧ Supplies for This Session ❧

- ☞ pens
- ☞ individual snack bags of trail mix (preferably a trail mix that includes a wide variety of items such as peanuts, almonds, raisins, M&M's, chocolate chips, sunflower seeds, dried cranberries, and so on). You'll need one bag of trail mix for each woman. (This can be your snack for the session.) **Make sure no one has any allergies, such as a nut allergy, before providing snacks.**
- ☞ research articles on the health benefits of friendship, one per small group (see the "Preparing for This Session" section)
- ☞ large pieces of paper or a dry-erase board and marker
- ☞ *Steel Magnolias* DVD (optional for "How Do We Do Better?" section)

❧ Preparing for This Session ❧

If you can't find a good trail mix at the local store, you can make your own trail mix and put it in individual plastic bags. You can include raisins, nuts, M&M's, and cereal.

Do a search on the Internet for research articles connecting friendship with health benefits. Here are some great sites to start with:

- www.anapsid.org/cnd/gender/tendfend.html
- http://health.ivillage.com/mindbody/mbhappy/0,,9t9dpn42,00.html
- www.heartinfo.org/ms/news/529452/main.html
- http://news.bbc.co.uk/2/hi/health/4094632.stm

Find three or four easy-to-read articles about what researchers/experts say regarding the health benefits of friendship. Use the words *research*, *friendship*, and *health benefits* in your search.

✎ *Enrichment for Leaders* ✎

Often we think of Paul as a hardcore, radically transformed Jesus follower who was incredibly zealous for the Lord. Which, of course, he was. But this week as you read Paul's words in Philippians, see Paul from a softer and gentler vantage point. Paul had a tender heart for being in committed relationships with other believers, and he found a lot of joy from his deep friendships. This session will focus on how we're called to do life together and how we can get better at living "shared" lives.

Slide 4.1

1. How Well Do You Share Life With Others?

Say: **Let's do a quick self-assessment and see how we're doing when it comes to doing life with others. I'm going to read a list of qualities in your Guidebook on page 33 that have been identified as key ingredients in building friendship. After I list the quality, rate yourself 1-10 on how well you do in this area of friendship. (1 being the worst; 10 being the best.)**

Pause after you read each word: **Supportive; Encouraging; Dependable; Self-Disclosing; Spiritually Concerned; Trustworthy; Compassionate; Loyal; Honest.**

Circle the two that were your highest. (Pause.) **Underline the two that were your lowest.** (Pause.)

2. Paul—A Man Who Shared His Life

Say: **Paul was really good at sharing his life with others. Much of his joy came from the joy he found in close friendships. Today we're going to look at a few verses he wrote to his close friends in Philippi and see what he can show us about becoming better at sharing our lives with other people.**

Have one of the women read out loud Philippians 1:7-9; 4:1; 4:14-16, which is printed in the Guidebook on page 34. As they're listening, have women circle in their Guidebook the word *you* and *your* every time they occur. Have them underline the words *my*, *me*, or *I*.

> *"So it is right that I should feel as I do about all of you, for you have a special place in my heart. You share with me the special favor of God, both in my imprisonment and in defending and confirming the truth of the Good News. God knows how much I love you and long for you with the tender compassion of Christ Jesus. I pray that your love will overflow more and more, and that you will keep on growing in knowledge and understanding." Philippians 1:7-9*

> *"Therefore, my dear brothers and sisters, stay true to the Lord. I love you and long to see you, dear friends, for you are my joy and the crown I receive for my work." Philippians 4:1*

> *"Even so, you have done well to share with me in my present difficulty. As you know, you Philippians were the only ones who gave me financial help when I first brought you the Good News and then traveled on from Macedonia. No other church did this. Even when I was in Thessalonica you sent help more than once." Philippians 4:14-16*

Say: **We can see that Paul cared deeply about the Philippians, and we also know that they were fervently devoted to Paul. The number of times we see "you" and "me" shows us how important relationships were to Paul.**

And this emphasis on relationships illustrates for us an underpinning truth of life as God intended: We were created to be in close relationship with others; we were made to share our lives with others.

Reread (or have another woman read) the verses using the Message translation. (Share with the women how the Message is a Bible translation using a more informal, everyday language style.)

"It's not at all fanciful for me to think this way about you. My prayers and hopes have deep roots in reality. You have, after all, stuck with me all the way from the time I was thrown in jail, put on trial, and came out of it in one piece. All along you have experienced with me the most generous help from God. He knows how much I love and miss you these days. Sometimes I think I feel as strongly about you as Christ does!

It was a beautiful thing that you came alongside me in my troubles. You Philippians well know, and you can be sure I'll never forget it, that when I first left Macedonia province, venturing out with the Message, not one church helped out in the give-and-take of this work except you. You were the only one. Even while I was in Thessalonica, you helped out—and not only once, but twice." Philippians 1:7-9; 4:1; 4:14-16, The Message

Say: **Again, we can see that Paul has poured his life and heart into these people, and they poured back into him. Let's dig into this idea of "sharing life" a little further in our own lives.**

Have women form their small groups. Hand out the bags of trail mix so each woman has a bag. Have them study the ingredients of the trail mix, and pick one of the pieces which represents them best. Ask them to share with their group what they picked and why. For example, someone who has a "nutty" sense of humor might choose a peanut.

Have the women discuss the "Sharing Life" Nudge Questions in their Guidebooks on page 35. Give the women about 15 minutes to discuss the Nudge Questions.

3. That Was Then; This Is Now

Say: **Let's examine what experts are saying about this idea of "shared" life.**

Still in their small groups, hand out one article to each group that you found regarding the health benefits of friendship and support. (If you have many small groups, it's OK for some groups to get the same article.) Have one woman in each group read the report to the others in her group, and then have each group work together to summarize the main points of their article. Give them around five minutes to do this.

After five minutes, have each small group present their findings to the large group. Write the findings on a dry-erase board or large piece of paper. Allow women to comment on similar findings or items from the research.

Conclude: **Research reveals that God's design for us to share our lives with others is a psychologically and physiologically healthier way to live.**

4. How Do We Do Better?

Say: **Now that we know how and why God wired us the way he did, how do we do it? How do we live in authentic relationships that fill our lives with God's joy? The first and most important aspect of shared lives is to have Christ be in the center of it. He needs to be in the center of our individual lives as well as the center of our Christian friendships.**

Slide 4.2

So what does this look like? How do we become like Paul and really learn to share our lives well with others and with Christ in the center?

Ask for seven volunteers to read out loud the Friendship Ideas listed in their Guidebooks on page 35. Ask the readers to read each idea slowly to the group.

1. Be intentional and committed; set a regular time and place to meet with a few friends who want to grow spiritually together. Make it a priority to be at the designated meeting times.

2. When you're together with close friends, be intentional in your conversation. Make sure each friend gets time to share what is going on in her heart and head. Get good at *listening* to each other.

3. Seek friends outside your stage of life. Find someone younger or older, with kids or without kids, working or staying at home; and then learn from each other!

4. Be a multi-tasker in your friendships, especially if your life is jam-packed and you can't find time to spend with friends. Do projects together once a month, such as painting bedrooms, reorganizing closets, cleaning cabinets, or exercising.

5. Pray together. Pray for each other. Find a prayer partner, and meet on a regular basis for prayer. Go on a regular prayer hike with friends. Pray together!

6. Go on weekend trips together. Going to a destination and spending multiple nights together is a great time to make memories and go deeper in friendship.

7. Learn to laugh together. A LOT! Life is so heavy that we need to turn it off sometimes and just laugh and be silly more often.

Ask: **What are some other ways we can do life together that you have experienced?** Brainstorm together, and write women's ideas on the white board or a large piece of paper. Have them write down some of their favorite ideas in their Guidebooks on page 36.

Looking over these ideas, what is one idea that strikes a chord with you? Circle that idea in your Guidebook. Challenge yourself to take a step in this area.

Now let's hear from a woman who's experienced the need for close friendships.

Helpful Hint ☞

If you want to drive this last suggestion home, show a clip from *Steel Magnolias*. Show the clip where M'Lynn (Sally Fields' character) is walking in her black funeral dress (after her daughter dies) with her friends all following her. It's a very sorrowful occasion, but when she says, "I just want to *hit* someone," her friends offer up Ouiser (Shirley MacLaine's character) as a punching bag. M'Lynn spontaneously breaks out into a giggle and laughter fills the moment. (This scene is about one hour and 45 minutes into the movie.)

Before this session, ask a woman from your group to share a story from her life about the joy she has found in close friendships. If there's not a woman from your group who can share, have a volunteer read the following story. Have this volunteer practice before the session so she can read with passion!

Lise

Here I am, trapped in this bewildering time of a woman's life called menopause. Actually, I'm not even there yet. My doctor tells me I'm only in peri-menopause, which are the months or years (depending on how lucky you are) that come before menopause. For every woman this time of life plays out differently, but I think I've experienced every possible

symptom—hot flashes, night sweats, irregular periods, and emotional rollercoaster rides. Did I mention my doctor told me that going through menopause is like being a teenager all over again? You can become a hormonal whack case. And some days that describes me perfectly.

I can deal with the night sweats by creating a mile-wide cavern in bed between me and my husband and throwing on and off the covers all night, but the hormone piece has been really hard for me. For the past year, I have watched myself, almost like an observer through a viewing glass, slip into depression. A thick, black cloud slowly descended onto my brain, making it very difficult for me to think clearly. To add to my misery, I began turning to a glass (or so) of wine every night, just to relax and numb myself. Of course this only made things worse because I hated myself for being so dependent on wine and would chastise and condemn myself every morning. But by the time late afternoon rolled around, I no longer cared about being a good Christian soldier. I just wanted my wine.

The dark cloud hovering over my brain shaded other areas of my life, too. I began pulling away from my girlfriends. And you have to know something about me—my girlfriends are like a pool of fresh spring water on a hot summer's day. They like me. They laugh at my jokes and think I'm really funny. They believe in me. They tell me the truth about myself. And, most importantly they point me toward God.

But in my depression, this truth became fuzzy. I started seeing myself as different from my girlfriends: Their kids seemed perfect; their husbands involved; their marriages intact; their parenting wise. So, I pulled away. They would call, wanting to go out for coffee, wanting to know how they could pray for me and support me. But I was too busy. Too much on my plate. I didn't want to be around them because in my mind I didn't measure up anymore.

This is no news flash—but doing life alone is lonely. I was lonely. Plus my depression-induced demented way of thinking became more demented because I no longer allowed my band of truth tellers inside. So the lies took root.

But just recently, in the last few months, there was a shake down in my

heart. The wall I built around myself started to crumble and then collapse as I saw how my girlfriends marched onward with me in spite of my withdrawal. They stepped in and prayed for me when I couldn't pray well for myself and held out hope for me when I had none. They believed for me. And, the clincher was they shared their lives with me. Their vulnerable hearts laid bare before me nudged at my soul, broke through the mound of lies I had told myself, and demonstrated to me all over again the deep need I have for sharing my life with a few trusted women.

It's not like this is a new lesson for me either. Years ago when I went through a long, weary season of infertility, I isolated myself. After coming out of the lonely infertile years, God showed me the better way to do life is with "my people" (as we fondly refer to each other). Why I had to relearn this I'm not sure. I guess depression mixed with Satan is a really bad concoction.

I've done life alone, and I've done life with others, and I deeply believe God doesn't want us to ride the rollercoaster solo. He meant for me to walk through my hills and valleys with my band of girlfriends. And through sharing life with them, I know joy in the deepest parts of my heart.

5. Wrap It Up

Say: **God created us to share our lives together. It's his design, and it's a good one. We can learn a lot from Paul and his friends in Philippi. They were in the thick of tough life together, and they were in it with Christ at the center. When we cultivate that kind of friendship, we'll multiply the joy God has for us.**

Close in prayer, thanking God for his gift of friendship and asking him to multiply it in your lives.

> *Announcement: Ask each woman to bring a woman's magazine, a pair of scissors, and a glue stick to next week's meeting.*

Joy Upside Down

✎ Supplies for This Session ✎

☞ poster board, 2 for every small group

☞ women's magazines

☞ scissors and glue sticks, about 1 glue stick and 1 pair of scissors for every three women

Even if you announced at the last session for women to bring magazines, glue sticks, and scissors, you'll want to supply some in case some forget.

☞ colorful markers

☞ sticky notes

☞ a branch or vine with smaller branches (or vines) shooting off of it

✎ Preparing for This Session ✎

If possible, seat the women in small groups at tables for today's session (with six or fewer women at each table). Put a poster board in the middle of each table with a stack of magazines and a few glue sticks and pairs of scissors. It's best if each woman can have her own magazine.

✎ Enrichment for Leaders ✎

This session concentrates on how secrets to joy are found in living like Christ, obedient and humble, versus the "Have It Your Way" attitude of our culture. It may seem like an upside down way to find joy—denying our own wants to obey Christ—but it's the surefire way to joy. As you prepare for this session, look around this week and notice all of the messages our culture sends telling us to live for "self."

1. Let's Take a Look

Have women go through the magazines and cut out advertisements that reveal our ME-centered culture and make a collage on their poster board. Allow 15 minutes for the women to cut and paste and make their collages. Put the collages on display on the walls, and have the women walk around to look at the displays.

On an empty table near the display, have sticky notes. Ask the women to put the sticky notes on those images or advertisements that "work"…the images and messages that make them feel like they do "deserve a break today" or that they should have it "their way" or that they are "worth it."

2. The Lie—"Me First" Brings Joy

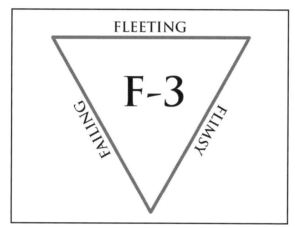

Slide 5.1

Have the women write the 3 Fs on their triangles in their Guidebooks on page 43. Then go through each F, and discuss it as a large group.

Ask:

- **How is the world's joy represented in these collages Fleeting?**

- **How is it Flimsy?**

- **How does it Fail us?**

After each question, allow the women an opportunity to answer the question and give examples. (Have some examples of your own to share, too.)

3. What Does God Say?

Read or have a volunteer read Philippians 2:2-8 out loud (it's printed in the Guidebook on page 43).

"Then make me truly happy by agreeing wholeheartedly with each other, loving one another, and working together with one mind and purpose.

Don't be selfish; don't try to impress others. Be humble, thinking of others as better than yourselves. Don't look out only for your own interests, but take an interest in others, too.

You must have the same attitude that Christ Jesus had.

Though he was God, he did not think of equality with God as something to cling to. Instead, he gave up his divine privileges; he took the humble position of a slave and was born as a human being. When he appeared in human form, he humbled himself in obedience to God and died a criminal's death on a cross." Philippians 2:2–8

Say: **In your Guidebooks, reread the verses to yourself. Underline one verse or part of a verse that particularly stands out to you. Write down your thoughts and reflections about what it says to you personally.**

(Give women a couple of minutes to do this.)

In their small groups, have women share what they underlined and wrote down. Have them also discuss the "Humility" Nudge Questions in their Guidebooks on page 44. Take about 10 minutes for this group time.

4. His Life: His Joy

Say: **When we live like Christ, we can know his joy.**

Read John 15:10-11.

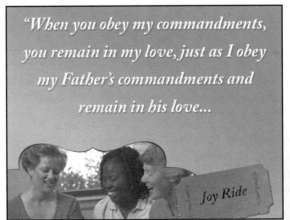

"When you obey my commandments, you remain in my love, just as I obey my Father's commandments and remain in his love...

Joy Ride

Slide 5.2

...I have told you these things so that you will be filled with my joy. Yes, your joy will overflow!"

John 15:10-11

Joy Ride

Slide 5.3

Say: There's a link between obedience and joy because when we obey, we "remain" in Christ. In our obedience, he then is the source of our joy.

Slide 5.4

Hold up your branch or vine.

When we're obedient, we "remain" in Christ, but when we choose disobedience, we become disconnected. (Snap off a side branch.) **He is the only source of true joy, so we need to "remain" in him in order to know and receive his joy. Let's hear a story that reflects this.**

Coffee Break

Before this session, ask a woman from your group to share a story from her life about a time she learned that disobedience to God is never a path to joy. If there's not a woman from your group who can share, have a volunteer read the following story. Have this volunteer practice before the session so she can read with passion!

Kamilia

Have you ever known the angst of not doing what you know God wants you to do? Of going right when you know he wants you to go left? I have. I was in my 30s, married, and a very committed Christian when I gave into the admiration and enticement of a man I worked with.

It started innocently enough. Daniel and I were on the same marketing team at a software corporation. We worked long hours together and our friendship grew. He was so attentive to me, always complimenting my work. Meanwhile, my marriage had grown a little flat. After seven years, I felt like my husband and I were more roommates than lovers.

One night Daniel and I were working late on an account presentation, and I made some derogatory remark about my body. He stopped typing on his laptop. "Don't say that. You're beautiful." He reached over and held my hand. "Your body is beautiful."

My heart leapt against my ribs, and my cheeks burned. I was speechless. I knew we were in a dangerous zone. I knew I needed to just laugh it off and keep working. But I didn't. I stared back into his eyes, and when he leaned in to kiss me, I let him.

That night when I drove home, I swung back and forth from guilt-ridden lows to heart-palpitation highs. I prayed fervently for God to

50

Rendezvous: JOY RIDE ❀ *PHILIPPIANS*

forgive me for what had just happened and asked him to help me stop what had started with Daniel. But the next day when I saw Daniel at work and he complimented my new outfit, I lost all my resolve.

For the next several months, I made a conscious decision to shelve God. I couldn't carry on with Daniel and still pray and read my Bible, like I'd always done. So I stopped. I dropped out of my Monday night Bible study, and almost every Sunday I made excuses to my husband about why I couldn't go to church. In order to live with myself, I had to shut God out of my mind.

My stolen moments with Daniel were just like you see in the movies—secret, romantic, and seemingly perfect. We never slept together, but we carried on a very flirtatious, emotional relationship. Then my husband found a note from Daniel tucked inside my purse. He was furious, but he also wanted to work on our marriage. I agreed. I never wanted a divorce. We met with our pastor, and he encouraged me to quit my job so I no longer would see Daniel every day. He said seeing Daniel would be too much strain on my already frail marriage. Our pastor said we were in crisis mode and my decisions at that point could make or break our marriage.

I was in agony. I hated myself for hurting my husband so much. The thought of losing my marriage was so painful. But the thought of saying goodbye to Daniel was painful, too. I decided to go away by myself for the weekend to think and pray. I went to a friend's cabin up in the mountains. Alone in the cabin, I turned and faced God for the first time in many months.

"I'm sorry," I whispered. "I'm so sorry. I know I have disobeyed you and disappointed you." The tears started flowing and didn't stop the whole weekend. Like the prodigal son, I wanted to be back with my father. I turned back to God, adhering myself to him once again. I drove home Sunday night and asked my husband for forgiveness. Monday morning I quit my job and said a tearful goodbye to Daniel.

That was 14 years ago. Looking back I've learned so much. My fling with Daniel seemed to bring joy at first, but only brought anguish and heartache in the end. I know when we make a conscious choice to disobey God, we cut ourselves off from the only real thing that satisfies… the only source of real lasting joy.

Say: **In your Guidebook on page 45, illustrate the timeline of your life. Mark different periods in your life when you were disobedient or held onto certain things you knew God wanted you to let go of. Examples might be times you sought out the "stuff" your friends or neighbors had, times you decided to live selfishly instead of choosing God, times you flirted when you knew you shouldn't, times you didn't forgive when you knew God wanted you to.**

After women have had several minutes to complete the timeline exercise, have them discuss the "Holding On" Nudge Questions on page 45 in their Guidebooks with their small groups. Give them 10 minutes for this.

5. Real Joy

Pass out another piece of poster board for each small group. Have the women create a new collage by going back through magazines and cutting out words and pictures that represent the words from Philippians 2:2-8. They can also use markers and write words on their collage this time. Give the women about 10-15 minutes to make their collage together.

Display the new collages next to the "world" collages. Encourage women to comment aloud on the noticeable differences between the collages.

6. Wrap It Up

Say: **These collages represent two very different messages. Paul's message to the Philippians in many ways takes the world's message and turns it upside down. It's in obeying God, not in obeying our own wants and desires, that we'll find true joy.**

Close together in prayer: **Lord, help us recognize how the world's message is so different from your message. Help us to be obedient as you were. Lord, show us the things in our lives that we hold onto and help us to let go of them. We want to know your joy as you promised us. Help us to find it through lives of obedience.**

Joy Inside Out

Supplies for This Session

☞ glass pitcher filled with water

☞ 7 foam cups with the names below written in large print with black permanent marker so each cup has one name: Timothy, Roman Palace Guards, Epaphroditus, Euodia, Syntyche, Lydia, New Christians in Rome

☞ small baggie for each woman with 5 sunflower seeds in their shells

Preparing for This Session

Put a table at the front of the room with the pitcher of water and the foam cups.

Enrichment for Leaders

This session highlights how joy is gathered and sustained through caring and doing for others. As you prepare for this week, reflect about a time in your life when you poured out your time and energy into another person because you felt God calling you to do it. If you feel like your "pouring out" experience is something that corresponds with this lesson, start the session by sharing your reflections on that experience and then move into the Philippians reading.

1. An Important Piece of Paul's Joy

Read or have another woman read Philippians 2:17-20.

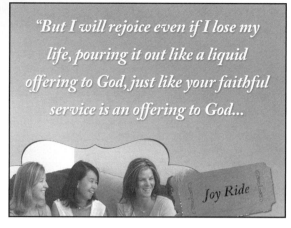

Slide 6.1

Slide 6.2

Say: Paul can't stop talking about joy in the first two verses of this reading. In your Guidebooks on page 49, circle every time Paul writes "joy" or "rejoice" in the first paragraph.

After the women finish circling the words in their Guidebook, read slide 3 out loud and then add:

It looks like a big joy festival for Paul…but what is the source of the joy?

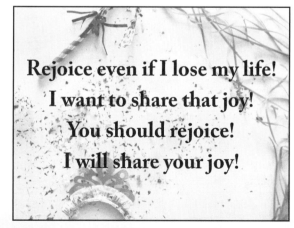

Slide 6.3

Give a minute for the women to reflect. Ask them to reread the verses, and then ask the question again:

What is the source of his joy here?

Allow the women to call out answers. Then reiterate that Paul's joy comes from pouring out his life into others as an offering to God.

At the front of the room, have a volunteer pour water from the glass pitcher into foam cups with the names of people Paul was pouring himself into. Make sure the names are facing forward, and explain that these are just a few of the people Paul poured his life into. You can read the names as the volunteer pours the water.

> *Say:* This pouring out of himself like a drink offering was an important source of Paul's joy. In your Guidebook on page 49, individually take a few minutes and do the "Pouring Out" exercise.

Allow about five minutes for this. Then have them join with a partner in answering the questions after this activity.

2. Paul's Role Model Is Jesus

> *Say:* Jesus said he didn't come to be served but to serve.

Read Matthew 20:28.

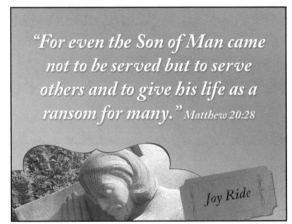

"For even the Son of Man came not to be served but to serve others and to give his life as a ransom for many." *Matthew 20:28*

Joy Ride

Slide 6.4

> Jesus came and poured out his life for us. He showed us how to live the life of a servant.

Have the women form small groups and discuss the "Servant" Nudge Questions in the Guidebook on page 50. Give them about 10 minutes for this. While they're involved in their group discussion, pass out the baggies of sunflower seeds.

Slide 6.5

After small groups are finished discussing, have women take the sunflower seeds out of the baggies, and ask:

How do we enjoy the sunflower seed?

Hold up a sunflower seed inside it's shell.

We take it out of it's shell. Right?

Open up a sunflower seed while you are saying this. Have the women open their sunflower seed shells, too. They can put the shells in the baggie and hold the sunflower seeds in their hand.

Now with the sunflower seed out of its shell, what can we do with it?

Allow time for the women to call out answers. Add to what they say if they don't cover everything.

• Eat it as a snack.

• Put it in a salad.

• Make sunflower oil out of it.

• Grind it and use it for cattle feed.

• Grind the seeds to make flour (Native Americans did this).

• Plant it for more sunflowers.

Read the "In Case You Wanted to Know" box.

> ### In Case You Wanted to Know
>
> *The little sunflower seed contains protein, poly-saturated and mono-saturated fats (the good fats that may protect your heart), folate, vitamin E, selenium (which works with vitamin E as an antioxidant), niacin, thiamin, calcium, iron, and magnesium.*

Have women eat the sunflower seeds (if they aren't allergic to them!) and think about all the vitamins they are ingesting!

Say: **The seed is inside the shell, and it needs to be opened up and taken out for us to enjoy.**

In their small groups, have women discuss the questions on slide 6.

Sowing Seeds of Joy

- How is Paul's "pouring out" of himself like the sunflower seed out of the shell?
- Why do you think joy comes from pouring ourselves out?
- When is a time you poured out your life into someone else and reaped joy?

Slide 6.6

Give the women about 10 minutes to discuss the questions, then get their attention and let them know it's time to hear from a woman who will share about her experiences related to pouring out joy.

Coffee Break

Before this session, ask a woman from your group to share a story from her life about a time she gained joy from pouring her life out to others. If there's not a woman from your group who can share, have a volunteer read the following story. Have this volunteer practice before the session so she can read with passion!

Charlotte

I used to be completely self-absorbed. Even though I became a Christian as a teenager, the idea of serving others never really registered with me. It wasn't what I thought about. I thought about how to make myself happy. What I wanted. What I needed.

I'm not making excuses, but the truth is this was how I was raised. My mother died four years after I got married, and I never once saw her volunteer or unselfishly give time to anyone. So, truthfully, the only paradigm I knew was: *Live for yourself.*

After I got married, my husband and I moved to a new city and found a church we both liked. There were a lot of young people our age there, and the pastor was warm and likeable. One Sunday they made an announcement that more people were needed to be greeters and hand out the Sunday morning programs. My husband and I wanted to meet more people, so we decided to volunteer two times a month. My motive was purely selfish. I saw it as an avenue to boost our social life.

I know it's pathetic, but that was the first time in my life I ever gave my time away, and I was so surprised by how much I enjoyed it. Who knew that smiling and handing out a program would be so fulfilling? I learned people's names. I answered their questions. I helped them find things. I asked them how they were doing. I had no idea how great it would feel to do something for other people.

A whole new world gradually opened up to me. I began to give more of my time without ulterior motives. I volunteered my organizational skills to women's ministry events. My husband and I helped church families move, and I brought meals over to new moms. Then I started volunteering outside the church at a shelter for runaway teens.

I'm not proud of this, but it took 10 years after I became a Christian before I discovered what Christ meant when he called us to serve others like he did. I still can't wrap my mind around the fact that he was God, and he washed his disciples' feet. But I know he calls me to do the same. To be humble. To give of myself even when I don't feel like giving.

The joy I've found in pouring myself into the lives of other people is something that's hard to explain. You know how you feel after you eat a really incredible meal? And you didn't eat too much so you're not uncomfortable. You ate the perfect amount, and it was delicious food. That is how my soul feels when I pour myself into another person who is in need. I walk away feeling full and wonderful.

But I also have to say that sometimes I see myself slipping back into my old ways and thinking more about myself than others. I have seasons where I have to just push through my old selfish and lazy patterns. And actually, it's those times—when I don't feel like giving but do anyway—that I'm blessed the most.

3. A Legacy We Can Learn From

Read out loud or have another woman read Philippians 2:19-22.

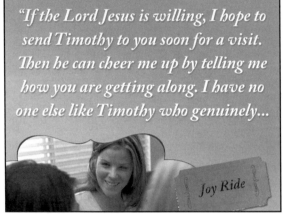

"If the Lord Jesus is willing, I hope to send Timothy to you soon for a visit. Then he can cheer me up by telling me how you are getting along. I have no one else like Timothy who genuinely...

Slide 6.7

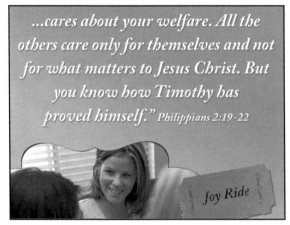

...cares about your welfare. All the others care only for themselves and not for what matters to Jesus Christ. But you know how Timothy has proved himself." Philippians 2:19-22

Slide 6.8

Say: **Out of all the men and women of faith in Paul's life, Timothy stands out. He is the only one who has genuine concern for others. He really cares…while others only care about themselves.**

Have the women think of a few people in their lives who take a genuine interest in them.

Ask: **What do they do that makes you know they have a genuine interest in you? Write this in your Guidebooks on page 50.**

Allow women a couple of minutes to write; then have them share with a small group what they wrote. After they've had time to share, ask volunteers

from groups to share some of the actions others take to show their genuine interest.

Then have the women decide one thing that was shared they'd like to do for one of their friends. Have them write this in their Guidebooks along with how they'll do it.

Say: These are ways we can become more like Timothy, taking genuine interest in others.

4. Play the "Follow Through" Game

Say: Often we have great intentions, but we lack follow through. We're going to play a game that gets us thinking more about following through with our good intentions.

Have the women pair off and read the rules to the game in their Guidebook on page 51. After they've read the instructions, ask if there are any questions. After any questions are answered, tell them you're going to time them, giving them one minute to fill in the blank dots. Remind them to be creative. Start the time with "on your mark, get set, go," and end the time with "Stop!"

Then allow about 10 minutes for the discussion that follows the game.

Game Rules

1. With your partner, find a common good intention you both have but haven't followed through on (such as visiting someone, helping someone, calling someone, saying you're sorry to someone, and so on).

2. Each of you write the good intention down at the "start" place in your own Guidebooks.

3. When the leader says "Go," each player writes down next to the dots one reason she didn't get her "good intention" done. (This filled-in dot is called a "barrier." Examples of barriers are: too busy, stressed out, scared, forgetful, car broke down, and so on.)

4. When the Leader says "Stop," put down your pen. Count how many barriers you came up with.

5. The "winner" is the one who has the most barriers. Now complete the discussion that follows in the Guidebook.

5. *Wrap It Up*

Read the story of the African Violet Lady (or have a volunteer read it).

> Once there lived a woman who suffered from depression and loneliness. She lived all by herself and had no friends or family. She rarely left her house or interacted with other people. A concerned neighbor tried to reach out to the lonely woman, but her efforts seemed futile. One day the worried neighbor heard about a very successful psychologist in their area who worked with lonely and depressed people. The neighbor called the psychologist and pleaded with him to make a house call on the depressed, lonely woman. The doctor was very busy, but because of the neighbor's tenacity, he finally agreed to make a visit.
>
> A week later when the psychologist visited the lonely woman, he was surprised by the utter chaos of her house. There was filth and clutter everywhere. She appeared to have let everything go to shambles, except for one thing—there were beautiful African violet plants in several rooms of the house. They had obviously been well taken care of because they were lush and thriving with big, purple blooms.
>
> After talking with the woman for a little while, the psychologist said, "I noticed that you have African violets. I can tell that you love flowers."
>
> The woman perked up a little bit and nodded, "Yes, I do."
>
> The psychologist said, "This is what I want you to do. I want you to grow more African violets. Make more seedlings from the plants you have and plant them in new pots. Then I want you to pick up your local newspaper every morning and look through the birth announcements and obituaries. Pick one person in your community who is either celebrating or grieving and bring that family one of your beautiful plants with a note from you."
>
> The lonely lady agreed. She began to grow more African violets and she poured over the newspaper every morning, looking for someone to

bring an African violet to. As she began to give to those around her, she discovered a purpose for her life.

Many years later when she died, hundreds of people came to her funeral. The church was packed as people celebrated the life of the well-known woman in their community known as the African violet lady.

Say: **This psychologist gave this lonely, depressed woman a prescription for joy. He told her to pour herself out into others.**

Let's heed that advice. Let's pour our lives out into others as Jesus modeled for us and Paul learned to do so well. The by-product is joy.

Close in prayer, asking God to help each woman to pour herself out in care and love for others.

Joy Back and Forth

❧ Supplies for This Session ❧

☞ song: "I Want to Be Where You Are" by Don Moen on the CD *Bless The Lord*

☞ a variety of props and costumes (funny hats, sunglasses, scarves, big coats, oversized overalls, traditional choir robes, tuxedo jackets, and so on)

☞ art supplies such as colored paper, felt pens, poster board, scissors, glue, yarn, felt, colored pipe cleaners

☞ large white board with pen (optional: laptop computer ready to project on screen)

☞ a worship team, an individual musician, or a CD player with familiar and favorite worship songs that focus on God in heaven and being with him. "I Can Only Imagine" by MercyMe is one song suggestion, but pick songs that fit the worship preferences of your group.

❧ Preparing for This Session ❧

On a large table, spread out all the props and costume items. On another large table, spread out the art supplies. Set up tables for each small group. They need to be large enough tables to comfortably work together on a project. Arrange for a worship team, worship leader or worship CD to be ready with two to three worship songs.

❧ *Enrichment for Leaders* ❧

It's time for a fresh focus. Yes, you were planning on putting together your plans for the next session with your women. But, before you do it, take a breather. Relax for a minute and exhale all the problems and stresses from your day. For a minute, force yourself to break away from thinking about your to-do list. Forget any current messes in your life or past mistakes that may be bogging you down. Pushing those things aside, focus on the truth of the hope in front of you! Focus on what's ahead of you—God's heavenly prize! A heavenly banquet with great food! No more headaches. No more messes. No more disappointments. Only rewards! And, best of all, God himself!

Can you imagine?

1. Whatever Is Past Is Past!

Start this week with your coffee break story time!

Before this session, ask a woman from your group to share a story from her life about a time she learned to put the past behind her. If there's not a woman from your group who can share, have a volunteer read the following story. Have this volunteer practice before the session so she can read with passion!

Brandy

I am a murderer. Worse, I murdered my own flesh and blood. How can I ever move on after what I've done? How can I ever accept God's forgiveness if I can't forgive myself? How in a million years could God ever really love me?

When I had my abortion, I was attending a Christian college. I was dating a really good-looking guy who was a leader in a large ministry on campus. I was sure I was in love with him. One night, back in my dorm room, we got carried away. He knew I didn't want to have sex before marriage, but all of a sudden he was on top of me and then it was over. I cried on and off for the next week. When I found out I was

pregnant a couple of months later, my whole world seemed to go black. I couldn't possibly tell my parents. And I didn't have any friends I felt safe confiding in. I did tell my boyfriend, and he encouraged me to have an abortion. So I did.

We broke up shortly after the horrific ordeal, and at night I began having the same bad dream over and over again. A baby was crying but I couldn't find it. In the dream, I'd run from room to room searching, feeling like I was getting closer to the baby. But I never found it. Every morning when I woke up, I'd beg God for forgiveness even though I knew what I had done was unforgivable.

Over time I stuffed the ordeal away in a dark closet inside my heart. It didn't resurface again until I got married several years later. Both my husband and I were eager to have children, but we didn't get pregnant right away. I started having the dream again. I also started to cry for no apparent reason. I'd be washing dishes after dinner and burst into tears. I'd cry in the shower and on my drive to work. I'd cry myself to sleep almost every night. I was a total mess and my husband had no idea how to help me.

Finally I confided my emotional misery to a friend of mine, Michelle, who also happened to be a high school counselor. She was amazing. She gently encouraged me to talk until I was ready to share with her what I had never told another soul. Not even my husband.

When I was 20-years-old, I had an abortion.

Michelle didn't blink an eye when I told her. There wasn't an ounce of judgment on her face, and she saw how stuck I was. She suggested we start taking walks together once a week before work. Over the next year of my life, we walked and talked and God's healing slowly took hold of my heart. Michelle showed me in the Bible what I couldn't see or believe for myself: God had forgiven me! She also showed me how God wanted *me to forgive myself.*

She told me, "If you don't forgive yourself, there will always be a huge barrier between you and God because you're always looking backward."

After many miles of walking, her words took root and grew inside me. It was like a spring rain shower in my soul after years of drought. I now know God has forgiven me. He was heartbroken when I was stuck in the past. He wants me to look forward. He wants my eyes glued on him and not on what's behind me. He wants me to run my race. And he wants me to run from a place of freedom because of what he's already done for me

on the cross. Yes, he died for even me, a woman who took the life of her own child.

So now I only look backward when I can minister to someone else who is stuck. I stop and show them where I've come from. Then I turn forward and show them where I am now—running a race toward eternity with Jesus at the finish line, arms opened wide, and calling out my name.

Say: **Wow! Thank you for that story. As we** *all* **probably know from personal experience, knowing God's joy comes when we can put our past behind us and focus on the grace God's given us. Let's take a few moments of silence to pray about any of our own experiences from the past this story brought to mind. I'll lead us in prayer after a minute.**

Be sensitive to where the women are at this moment. Lead in prayer, thanking God for his mercies that are new every morning; thanking him for forgiveness that is real; thanking him for peace that allows us to move forward with joy! Pray for the time together, that all of the women would be able to fully embrace their futures because of the time spent together.

2. What's Your Target?

Have a volunteer read this quick story.

Slide 7.1

Target Practice

A man went out to the backyard every night to use his archery equipment. Every night. Faithfully. His neighbor noticed him doing this every evening and started wondering if the guy was any good. So one evening, the neighbor walked over to watch the archer. The archer stopped what he was doing and greeted his neighbor. The neighbor said,

---

"Hey, I see you practicing every evening, and I'm just wondering if you're any good at this. I'd be interested in learning." The archer went over to his stack of targets and handed the pile to his neighbor. The neighbor began looking through the pile—bull's eye, bull's eye, bull's eye. Every single paper had just one hole in it. Always a bull's eye. "How do you do it?" the neighbor inquired. "It's easy," said the archer, "I shoot the arrow first and then I draw my target."

Say: Wouldn't it be a whole lot easier in life if we could draw in our target *after* we act, like this man did? Unfortunately, it doesn't work like that in real life. We need to make a conscious decision about what our target will be in life. Paul was a man who knew exactly what he was aiming for.

Have the women turn in their Guidebooks on page 57 and read Philippians 3:10-17. Have them write two or three bullet points that summarize the passage. You can have the women work alone or with a partner.

"I want to know Christ and experience the mighty power that raised him from the dead. I want to suffer with him, sharing in his death, so that one way or another I will experience the resurrection from the dead!

I don't mean to say that I have already achieved these things or that I have already reached perfection. But I press on to possess that perfection for which Christ Jesus first possessed me. No, dear brothers and sisters, I have not achieved it, but I focus on this one thing: Forgetting the past and looking forward to what lies ahead, I press on to reach the end of the race and receive the heavenly prize for which God, through Christ Jesus, is calling us.

Let all who are spiritually mature agree on these things. If you disagree on some point, I believe God will make it plain to you. But we must hold on to the progress we have already made.

Dear brothers and sisters, pattern your lives after mine, and learn from those who follow our example." Philippians 3:10–17

After about six minutes, ask for volunteers to share what they wrote. Write their summaries on a large white board or have someone type them into a laptop, for projection, as they read their summaries.

Say: **Paul knew his target in life. He said "I want to *know* Christ." In the Amplified Bible, an important word is often defined and expanded upon. In Philippians 3:10, the Amplified Bible reads:**

(Read the verse from the slide.)

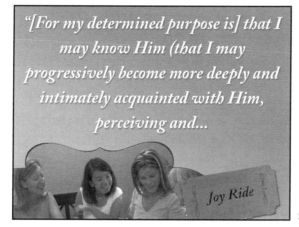

"*[For my determined purpose is] that I may know Him (that I may progressively become more deeply and intimately acquainted with Him, perceiving and...*

Joy Ride

Slide 7.2

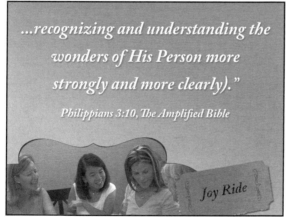

...recognizing and understanding the wonders of His Person more strongly and more clearly)."

Philippians 3:10, The Amplified Bible

Joy Ride

Slide 7.3

Ask: **What's the difference between *knowing about* and *knowing* someone?**

(Allow time for a variety of responses. *Knowing about* is intellectual and could be very distant; *knowing* is relational and is close.)

Say: **Paul didn't want to know *about* Christ. He wanted to *know* Christ. As the Amplified Bible's translation of this verse shows, to Paul knowing Christ meant an intimate, deep, growing relationship with him. That was Paul's focus, and he didn't let his mistakes in the past get in the way.**

Ask someone to read verse 14 out loud.

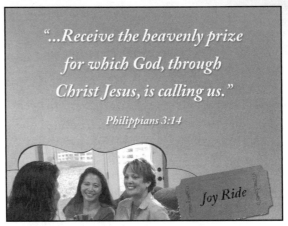

Slide 7.4

Ask: **What do you think the heavenly prize Paul is talking about here is?**

(Allow women to offer several answers.)

Say: **Paul says the prize is *heavenly*, but the prize isn't just heaven. God himself is the prize! Eternity in heaven with *him*!**

3. How Do We Aim for the Right Target?

Say: **There are two important elements to reaching our target of an intimate relationship with Christ. The first is *to forget*. Paul tells us in verse 3:12 he hasn't attained perfection but he presses forward toward Christ. How does he do this? Two ways. First, he chooses to forget (which means to not focus on) what he's done in the past *because it takes his eyes off Christ*.**

Slide 7.5

Have women get into small groups and discuss the "Forget" Nudge Questions on page 58 of the Guidebook. Give them about 10 minutes to discuss.

Say: **The second element to reaching our target is *to focus*. Not only did Paul *not* look back at his mistakes; he changed his focus to what was ahead of him. He *did* look ahead at his goal.**

Give women about five to 10 minutes to do the "Focus" Nudge Questions in their Guidebooks on page 59.

Then say:

Let's take some time right now to focus on our target—being with God, in his presence.

Play or have someone sing the song: "I Want to Be Where You Are" by Don Moen.

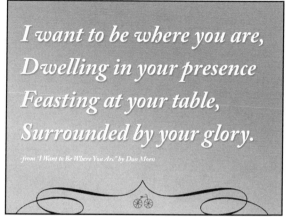

I want to be where you are,
Dwelling in your presence
Feasting at your table,
Surrounded by your glory.

from "I Want to Be Where You Are" by Don Moen

Slide 7.6

After the song, remind women that we find joy when we focus on our future—being with God in heaven.

In small groups, have women use the variety of props and costumes and art supplies to imagine and prepare something to share with the whole group that *depicts being with God in heaven.* This can be something they create from the art supplies, something they create from the props, something they demonstrate with a drama, something they write and illustrate, and so on. Let the women know they should have fun with this. It doesn't need to be all somber and serious.

Tell the women they have 15 minutes for this group activity and then you'll come back together as a large group.

4. Sharing Through Worship

With a worship team or CD, have two to three very familiar worship songs ready to sing together once you've regrouped. Intersperse the worship music with the groups sharing their depictions of being with God in heaven. Make sure you applaud after each group shares!

5. Wrap It Up

Have your group leader or worship leader close with a final heaven-oriented worship song and prayer. Have her also pray that God would help the women to have one focused goal, their pursuit of knowing him, and that he would help them forget the past and strive on toward their joy in him.

Helpful Hint

Even if your group is a small home group, this is a great project to do in mini-groups of two.

The Peace-Joy Package

❧ Supplies for This Session ☙

☛ one small sticky note or slip of paper per woman

☛ pens

☛ markers

☛ scissors

☛ tape or glue

❧ Preparing for This Session ☙

Set up tables with enough supplies for each woman to be able to work at the same time without having to wait: scissors, markers, tape or glue. Have two readers well rehearsed and ready with the two readings.

❧ Enrichment for Leaders ☙

Have you ever been stuck in a cycle of stewing…festering…in a slow rot? Repeating over and over again whatever it was that happened—the mean words someone said, the meeting you weren't included in, the memo that's got you worried? Talk yourself through Philippians 4:8.

"And now, dear brothers and sisters, one final thing. Fix your thoughts on what is true, and honorable, and right, and pure, and lovely, and admirable. Think about things that are excellent and worthy of praise."

"Girl, is there anything true in your thinking?" *I don't know.* "Anything honorable?" *Probably not.* "Anything right?" *Not really.* "Anything pure?" *No.* "What about lovely or admirable or excellent or praiseworthy?" *No on all counts.* "Then, sister, you are totally wasting your time!"

Reflect on this process this week as you prepare for this session that focuses on trading our worry for God's peace by giving every concern and request to God.

1. Worry Warts

Say: Worry is like a rocking chair—there's a whole lot of movement, but you don't get anywhere. Not very much of what we worry about really ends up happening. So, why do we spend so much time doing it?

Slide 8.1

Give each woman a sticky note or slip of paper. Tell them to list *everything* they can think of that they've worried about in the past week on this piece of paper. Then tell them to hang onto it for later.

Helpful Hint ☞

If you have a rocking chair available, introduce this session while you're sitting and rocking in a rocking chair yourself.

2. Anxiety Busters

Read together Philippians 4:6.

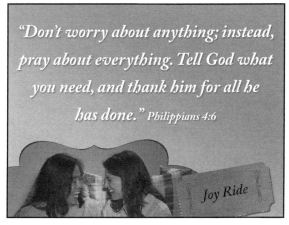

"Don't worry about anything; instead, pray about everything. Tell God what you need, and thank him for all he has done." *Philippians 4:6*

Joy Ride

Slide 8.2

Helpful Hint ☞

Throughout today's session, while women are working on lists or in small group time, play Bobby McFerrin's "Don't Worry, Be Happy" for fun ambience.

Say: There's no option here. God doesn't say, "You don't *have* to worry; you *could* do something else." He says *"Don't!* Don't worry about anything!"

Ask: What are some phony, failing ways to try to not worry?

(Allow the women time to answer. Add to the responses: denial, trying to stay busy with something else, taking a nap, working out at the gym, and so on.)

Say: These aren't all bad options; they just don't work long term. The *only* long-term solution is the only option God gives us for worry—prayer!!

Have someone read Philippians 4:6-9 from their Guidebooks on page 65.

> *"Don't worry about anything; instead, pray about everything. Tell God what you need, and thank him for all he has done. Then you will experience God's peace, which exceeds anything we can understand. His peace will guard your hearts and minds as you live in Christ Jesus.*
>
> *And now, dear brothers and sisters, one final thing. Fix your thoughts on what is true, and honorable, and right, and pure, and lovely, and admirable. Think about things that are excellent and worthy of praise. Keep putting into practice all you learned and received from me— everything you heard from me and saw me doing. Then the God of peace will be with you." Philippians 4:6-9*

Say: Let's look more closely at this prayer directive. It's not a formula, but it has important elements that can help us be more effective in our prayer.

Have the women move to tables with the artwork items on them. Have women cut out the page in their Guidebooks with a cube on it on page 71.

Slide 8.3

Say: One of the first directives in Philippians 4:6-9 is "pray about everything." God wants us to come to him with *everything*. Nothing is too big or too small. He wants it all.

Instruct the women to label one of the four sides of their cube "pray about everything."

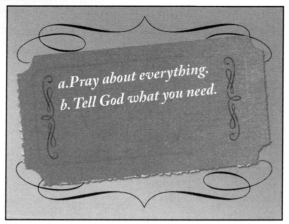

Slide 8.4

Say: **A second directive is "tell God what you need."**

Instruct the women to add "Tell God what you need" to another side of the cube.

Other translations say "petition" or "supplication." This means we should be specific about what is on our hearts and minds. God already knows, but sometimes he wants us to tell him—it fosters our relationship with him. He wants us to humble ourselves enough to admit we can't do life on our own.

Give an example of what this looks like, or use this example. Parents know the desire to be asked for things by their children—they are excited about doing something for their child, but they wait. They wait for their children to get to a place to ask. The child tries to pick up something that's too heavy to lift. The parent waits, quietly, a small smile appearing on her face, as the child finally turns and says, "Mommy, hep me, peeze!"

Slide 8.5

Say: **The next directive in this passage is to thank God. Thank him for all he has done.**

Instruct the women to add "Thank God" to another side of the cube.

Say: Cultivate an attitude of gratitude. Never just ask for something. Always remember to thank God for what he's already done. He doesn't need our thanks, but we need to give it. It helps *our* perspective!

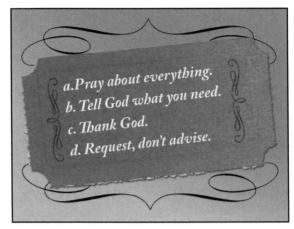

Slide 8.6

Lastly, always remember to give God your requests, *not* your advice.

Instruct the women to add "Request, don't advise" to the fourth side of the cube.

Too many times we advise God. For example, we don't just give God our request for our sister to grow closer to God. We advise God with something like this:

Have a woman ready to read this mini drama. (Make sure she uses a know-it-all tone in her prayer!)

> "God, bring a new Christian worker to my sister's office. Help this woman be friendly to my sister. You could even bring in two dynamic Christian women into her office. That would be even better! And make sure they're interested in gardening; she likes gardening. And then it would be great if the house for sale across her street was bought by a Christian family. Not just average Christians—really dynamic Christians. Oh, and make them people my sister would relate to. That would be so great, God. If I were you, that's what I would do."

Say: Maybe we don't sound quite like this. But in our own way, we do this sometimes, don't we?

Instruct the women to finish their cubes by writing a personal reminder to themselves on the top of the cubes—it could be a short note or a symbol that

has significance to them. Then have them cut out and glue or tape the cube together.

Have women return to their seats. Review the four sides of the prayer cube with them.

> *Say:* **When you're praying, you can just say "Here, God!" and hand him your cube. "Here's what my heart is heavy about. Please take care of it. I'm leaving it with you."**

Have women take the sticky notes they wrote their worries on earlier and put them in the cube.

> **Take this cube home and use it as a guide to your prayer. Each day, you can write down on slips of paper what you need or what your worries are, just like you did on the sticky notes today. Then put these needs in your cube, and hand them over to God. When we entrust our needs to God in prayer, God uses our prayers to replace our worry with peace.**

Lead the group in a time of prayer, giving all of the worries they put in their boxes to Christ. You could also allow women a short time of personal prayer. Then let women know it's time to hear the story of a woman who has learned about dealing with worry first-hand.

Before this session, ask a woman from your group to share a story from her life about a time she learned to not worry but have God's peace. If there's not a woman from your group who can share, have a volunteer read the following story. Have this volunteer practice before the session so she can read with passion!

Sharon

As I'm writing this, I'm in Nigeria living in a camp of expatriates—men and women who are internationals. I'm here because my husband, Jim, accepted a job reassignment with the oil-related company he works for. We are new empty-nesters and were very excited about this opportunity

to live in another country, a needy country. After praying a lot, we knew it was what God wanted us to do. What I didn't know was how hard it was going to be.

After we arrived almost a year ago, the camp was put on lock down because internationals in the oil industry were regularly being kidnapped. Now we can only leave the compound for essential travel with a police escort. Almost all of our time is spent inside the barbed-wire-topped walls with guards at the gate 24/7. And it's a small space.

The only ones in the camp who are Christians are some of the Nigerians, and their culture is so corrupt that following Christ really has no affect on their behavior. Lying, cheating, and basic laziness are everyday occurrences for those who proudly say they're off to a meeting at church! I have found myself desperately lonely for Christian community—people I can trust and pray with.

The food and housing is another challenge. When we arrived, we faced a disgusting mold problem that was in the carpets, the wardrobes, and on the bathroom walls. The local foods are difficult to get down without gagging, and finding food we are accustomed to is sometimes impossible.

Recently I was hired into a liaison position in the camp to create opportunities for the families moving here to have the best possible experience while they're here. I saw this job as a wonderful avenue to make a difference in the lives of people with the love of Christ. But this has proven to be another tremendous challenge—I spend most of my day listening to people complain. When one woman arrived at my apartment at 7:00 a.m. to complain about the color of her couch, I finally posted a sign at my door reminding people that I have an office with office hours.

The challenges of my job, the food, the housing, the lock down, and the lack of Christian fellowship have been testing and sometimes even exciting because I've been stretched outside of my culture. But there is one hardship over here that is nothing but hard—really, really hard. There's a small group of women living in the camp who hate me. I mean truly hate me with a level of vengeance I've never seen before. Part of why they hate me is because I'm a Christian. Another reason is I was

voted into a volunteer leadership role that one of the women wanted. And then I was hired for this job that another woman in the group wanted. They act out their hate in a lot of different ways including gossip, making up lies about me, and just being downright nasty to me.

I now see how much easier it is to have "peace" when you live in a safe place, are surrounded with loving Christian friends, and your physical needs are not a daily challenge. But I've been pushed outside of those comforts. And I know what Paul is saying when he tells the Philippians to guard their hearts and minds because over here the voices, circumstances, and my own weariness could easily suck me into a vortex where I wouldn't hear God or experience what he wants to give me. Just like pollution can ruin a clear blue day, unprotected thoughts can wreak spiritual havoc.

I've found that when I get away and remove myself from the nasty words and ongoing complaints, God does something amazing! Alone with God, I sit down and pour out my heart, laying at his feet my burdened, weary, empty, sad, and scared self. I don't hold back or skimp at all. I just let it all out. It's like balm being gently rubbed over a wound. Solace slowly slips in, and he takes my heavy sack of woes and trades it for his peace.

In Nigeria, I've experienced anew how God gives me something no one else and nothing else can give: a joy that makes no sense and a peace that transcends.

3. The Peace of God

Move the women into their small groups. Using their Guidebooks, give them 10-15 minutes to discuss the "Worry Trade" Nudge Questions on page 66. Then invite them back to the large group.

Say: **If we read our passage for today again, Philippians 4:6-9, we'll see that God doesn't just tell us *not* to worry, he tells us what to do instead. Let's reread the end of this passage.**

> *"And now, dear brothers and sisters, one final thing. Fix your thoughts on what is true, and honorable, and right, and pure, and lovely, and admirable. Think about things that are excellent and worthy of praise. Keep putting into practice all you learned and received from me— everything you heard from me and saw me doing. Then the God of peace will be with you." Philippians 4:8-9*

This passage doesn't just say, "don't worry," it tells us what to do instead— think about what is true, honorable, right, and pure. We should replace our worrisome thoughts with the kinds of things God wants us to talk about.

Turn in your Guidebooks to the "Fix Your Thoughts" section on page 66. God wants us to *fix* our thoughts on what is true. If we're worrying about our finances, the truth that God wants us to fix our minds on might be that he will always take care of us. Take a minute now to write a truth you think God wants you to focus on instead of one of your current worries.

Give women a minute to write. Do this with each of the bullets in their Guidebooks on page 67 (*true, right, pure, lovely,* and *admirable.*) You might want to give examples. For example, if they're worrying about a friendship in which a friend has offended them, they might write down to have only admirable thoughts of that friend.

4. Wrap It Up

Say: **God doesn't just send peace our way—he, himself, is with us! So we can have the peace of God *and* the God of peace.**

Close with a short prayer.

Thank you, Father, for this amazing peace and for the joy that comes with it. Thank you that you offer it to us, Lord. Help us to receive it!

Helpful Hint

Look ahead to Session 10 for some preparations you'll want to start thinking about.

Glad Surrender

☙ Supplies for This Session ❧

☞ song: "Trading My Sorrows" by Darrell Evans on *Set Free* or *Spirit and Song 2 Vol 9*

☞ TV studio props with a daytime talk show look—couches, tables, home décor, bright lights

☙ Preparing for This Session ❧

At least two weeks before this session, work with two women: 1) a woman who will be "Pauline," a modern-day, Paul-like woman and 2) a woman who will be a talk show host. The talk show host needs to be good with impromptu quips that will cause audience reactions. The "Pauline" character needs to have her lines well rehearsed and almost memorized. Set up the stage like a TV studio, talk show format, with the large group serving as the live audience.

Also, pre-arrange for readers to read each of these passages, loudly, from their seats: Psalm 23:1-4; 18:1-2; 16:8; 30:1-3; 32:7-8; 34:4-6; and 37:4-7. (These passages are printed in their Guidebooks.)

☙ Enrichment for Leaders ❧

Ever gotten caught in this trap: "If I had what *she* has…then I'd be happy"? Much too often we depend on our circumstances to make us happy. This session challenges us to let go of dependence on our circumstances for our happiness. Consciously consider during this time of preparation any large and small ways you can surrender to God and allow him to be your source of joy by admitting you don't have the ability to manufacture joy on your own.

1. Set the Stage

After welcoming the women, invite them to turn to page 73 in their Guidebooks and list the top five things about their life that they complain about the most or are most unhappy about.

Allow about four to five minutes for them to think and write.

> **Say:** We'll get back to your complaints a little bit later. Today, we're privileged to be a part of a live studio audience as we are watching the live production of "The _____ Show!"

(Use the real name of the woman who plays the part of the talk show host.)

An Interview With "Pauline," a Modern-Day Paul

(The talk show host carries the dialogue, filling in with impromptu thoughts as needed.)

Host: I'm so glad you all came to see our show today. Please join me in giving Pauline a warm welcome. *(Pause for applause.)* Pauline, we've read your letters, and we are, quite frankly, speechless at the thought of having you here with us today.

Pauline: Thank you, [host's real name.] It's my privilege to be here.

Host: Pauline, first of all, I know you don't like to boast, but could you tell our audience a bit about your credentials?

Pauline: Early in my life, I was very close to perfect. I obeyed all laws. I even added in extra laws just to be able to show that I could keep every law, no matter how tough. I was a leader of leaders. I had incredible zeal and passion about what I did. I really made it tough on Jesus followers back then. I tried to get them thrown out of our community. They just didn't fit in. We had a covenant-controlled community, of course, and they didn't maintain the covenants. I tried to get them arrested. Often, I succeeded.

Host: Allow me to interrupt for a moment, Pauline. You actually had the Jesus followers arrested? Why?

Pauline: They weren't following all of the laws. Here's an example—we clearly said all homes in our community had to have exterior paint colors of either beige, white, or pale yellow. I was shocked when one family started painting their house with blue paint. And, worse yet, they were painting on a Sunday! We were appalled.

Host: Shocking.

Pauline: But that was before.

Host: Before?

Pauline: Before my walk that amazing day.

Host: Really? What happened?

Pauline: Well, I thought I was serving God. I thought he would be pleased with how well I obeyed the laws. I thought he would be impressed with me because I came up with some laws that he hadn't even thought of. I thought…well, it doesn't matter what I thought…I was wrong. He showed up one day while I was walking down the road. He showed up in an amazing way. I had an encounter with the true and living God, and it changed my life. My name was even changed. I had been known as Sauline before that day. No one remembers that now…I even forget…my life is so different now. I'm really not the same person I was then. Thanks to Jesus.

Host: Please tell us more.

Pauline: Well, from that day on, all of my passion and zeal has been focused on serving the living God. Jesus is my whole reason for living because believe me, I'd rather be dead.

Host: (Stunned) What?

Pauline: Well, I don't mean that I'm so miserable that I want to die. It's just that to be gone from here would mean I'd be with Jesus…*(wistfully and with sincerity)* and there's no greater thing! That's why I say that Jesus is my whole reason for living. I wouldn't be here if it weren't for him.

Host: So, that's where your joy comes from? Jesus? He must have made your life really terrific, huh?

Pauline: Oh, yes! But not in the ways you would think. My circumstances have, well, they've been pretty bad. Beaten. Tortured. Imprisoned. Beaten some more. The danger from my own community is astounding. I have to be constantly on the move or else I'll be arrested again or killed. I've been in major car accidents where I shouldn't have survived. I've been hungry and homeless. I've been without clothes or money.

Host: Wait a minute. This is astounding! You've been through all that?

Pauline: Yes. Actually that's not even all of it. But you see, it doesn't matter what happens in my day. Sometimes I'm treated to great feasts. Sometimes I'm starving. Sometimes I've got the best 4,000 square foot house in the neighborhood. Sometimes I'm homeless. Sometimes I'm surrounded by friends. Sometimes I am alone, isolated. But those things don't define me or dictate my life. Everything around me can change but God gives me strength and joy—and that never changes.

Host: You say it like you mean it.

Pauline: Believe me, this is not something to joke about. I have learned the secret of being content. Circumstances can change every day. Contentment, well, contentment is much bigger than my circumstances.

Host: Bigger? …Oh, I'm sorry. Our time got away from us. That's it for today.

I'm [host's real name], and we invite you back tomorrow for another exciting interview. We will be meeting a woman who, as an orphan, was kidnapped out of the home of her cousin. She spent one year in training so she could qualify for a beauty contest. Join us tomorrow for an interview with Esther.

2. *Under the Circumstances*

Read Philippians 4:11-13 together.

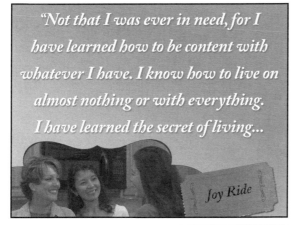

Slide 9.1

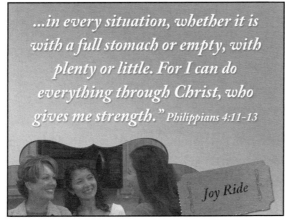

Slide 9.2

Say: **Have you ever asked someone how they're doing and they say, "Well, under the circumstances, I'm doing just fine!"**

You could, if you knew them well, scrunch down and peer under an imaginary table and say, "What are you doing down there? Under the circumstances?"

(Crouch down and act this out as you are saying it. Then stand up and continue.)

Don't get *under* the circumstances! That's letting life control you.

Ever wonder how two people can go through the same set of negative circumstances—one comes out fine and the other stays down—under the circumstances.

Slide 9.3

Say: The secret is geometrical. Are you living vertically? Or are you living horizontally? Let's see.

Ask the women to stand up and spread out around the room. Have them lie down on the floor, flat on their backs. Be sure you participate too!

Are you anchored to earth, horizontally, by life's circumstances? Stuck there, pulled down by gravity?

While they are still lying there, ask them to close their eyes and fill in the blank to this sentence (silently). "I'd be more content if _____."
Repeat the question and give them a minute to think.

Now, instruct everyone to stand. Have them reach for the sky, looking upward. Allow time for everyone to join.

Or, instead of being anchored down by life's circumstances, are you hanging on to heaven? Are you doing life vertically, depending on God's power and strength?

While women are standing there, have them fill in the blank to this sentence (silently). "God, thank you for the joy I find in _____." Have the women return to their seats.

Explain how Paul had learned the joy of living vertically, unbound by circumstances that could make or break his contentment. There was no "if only" to his contentment.

3. The Learning Curve for Contentment

Reread verses 11 and 12:

"For *I have learned* how to be content with whatever I have. I know how to live on almost nothing or with everything. *I have learned* the secret of

living in every situation, whether it is with a full stomach or empty, with plenty or little" (emphasis added).

Say: Notice the important words in this passage: It says twice, "I have learned." You and I don't inherit this ability to be content as soon as we become Christians. It's a progressive thing. It's a process. It was for Paul and it is for us. Let's hear from a woman who learned this secret of being content.

Coffee Break

Before this session, ask a woman from your group to share a story from her life about a time she learned contentment. If there's not a woman from your group who can share, have a volunteer read the following story. Have this volunteer practice before the session so she can read with passion!

Jodie

I had it all. Or at least all I'd ever dreamed of. A beautiful, sprawling house. Two beautiful children. A devoted, faithful Christian husband. A great church and lots of friends. Our home was over 6,000 square feet in the middle of a gorgeous 2-acre wooded lot. My favorite thing to do was sit on my back veranda and look out over our gardens. I would curl up on the chaise lounge, admiring the beauty and lapping up all the blessings God had given us.

But all this changed when my husband was sued. The CFO in his company embezzled money and conducted other illegal business and my husband, as CEO, was taken down with him. The CFO went to prison, and we lost everything.

Hmm…how do I describe my emotions as I packed up our house and said goodbye to my beautiful things? (They even got my wedding ring!) Was I angry? Yes. Bitter? Yes. Depressed? Yes. Embarrassed? Yes. I felt like I was in the middle of a really bad dream and kept trying to wake myself out of it. But it was real. And I was awake.

We moved into a tiny apartment, and I hated it. I mean I *loathed* it. How could this have happened? Why would the Lord take our home where we held so many Bible studies and church meetings? Then, to heap more misery over my life, we found out my husband had cancer in his sinus cavity. Due to intense chemo and several surgeries, he was unable to work for over a year. We sank further down the financial ladder, and now we were literally on the poverty threshold. I had to go ask our church for help. It was so humiliating, and I found myself growing angrier each day.

One afternoon when I was at the grocery store, just standing in line, I pulled out a news magazine and started reading an article about a rash of forest fires in California. I gazed at a picture of an older woman holding the hand of a young girl. The woman had bright blue eyes that stood out on her weathered old face. Underneath the picture it read, "A victim of California's latest fire loses her home where she has resided for the past 58 years."

Compelled to know more of her story, I pulled my grocery cart back and stepped out of line. I skimmed the article until I got to a question asked by the journalist: "You seem to be remarkably OK, based on your circumstances. How come?"

"Well it's a choice. I could be mad at God for allowing my home to be taken, or I could accept it and trust him. But either way, my home is gone."

The old woman's answer seared my heart. I stood staring at the picture of her for a long time. The article didn't say it, but I knew by her eyes what choice she had made. She had accepted it and trusted God.

My throat felt tight as I put the magazine back in the rack. *God, I want to be like her*, I prayed. *I want to trust you in all my circumstances not just when things are going well.*

It has been over 10 years since we lost everything. On my own strength, I know I would still be a bitter, angry woman. But I don't try to do it on my own. I lean into God. I count on his strength and his perspective. It has been a process, but I am a very different person today. I find joy in everyday little things. I am actually content with our small apartment and, on really good days, I find it cozy and charming. Best of all, I have

discovered a new dependence on God that draws me intimately close to him in a way I never experienced when I had it all.

4. The Source of Contentment

Say: **We can't paste a smile on our face and say, "I'm joyful!" We cannot just force ourselves to be content. That kind of attitude can only come from God. God gives us the strength to go through each day, whether it's a day filled with wonderful surprises or a day filled with heavy sorrows. Either way, we *can* be content.**

Have the pre-arranged readers read loudly from their seats the following passages from the Psalms: Psalm 23:1-4; 18:1-2; 16:8; 30:1-3; 32:7-8; 34:4-6; and 37:4-7. (These are printed in their Guidebooks starting on page 73.)

Instruct the women to move into their small groups. Allow them 10-15 minutes to discuss the "Contentment" Nudge Questions in their Guidebooks on page 75.

5. Wrap It Up

Say: **After sharing times when we've experienced God's strength, it seems like a no-brainer to always trust God. But most of us struggle with control issues.**

Amazingly, the one we are least likely to give control to is the one who is most able to handle our situations—God, himself! Accepting the fact that we aren't God and letting God be God is one of the toughest of human dilemmas.

Have each woman stand and hold out her hands in front of her. Instruct the women to make tight fists with both hands and keep them tight until you tell them to stop. Tell them they need to really squeeze hard.

So often in life we are gripped with fear, fear that we can't control our lives. So we tighten our grip on the things we think we can control.

(Remind them to keep their fists tight.)

And we become strong, self-sufficient women—or at least we like to look that way. We grit our teeth and clench our fists and we force ourselves to move forward—all in our own strength. Keep those fists tight. We say, "I can do this. I'm going to do this." And we exhaust ourselves by striving even harder. There's nothing about this that looks like joy!

We want to trust God. We know we should. The toughest part is the very beginning of our attempts to let go.

Have the women open their hands and wiggle their fingers. They will feel some pain as they are loosened. Tell them to turn their hands over and gently shake them out, palms down.

Here comes the other tough part!

Have the women flip their hands over with their palms up.

This is surrender. This is coming to God with nothing, no strength, no wisdom. Nothing to boast about, absolutely nothing. We come to him and humbly say, "God, here I am. I've got nothing to offer you except my open hands. Fill them, Lord. Give me your strength."

It's a choice. Sometimes we make it daily. Sometimes, for some of us who tend to be more stubborn, we make these choices by the minute. It's a conscious choice to trade our troubles for God's joy.

Close your time together with prayer. Before the women leave, have a woman sing or play the recording of Darrell Evans' song: "Trading My Sorrows."

Rejoice! It's All About Him!

❧ Supplies for This Session ❧

☞ room decorations that create a festive, joyous atmosphere

☞ round tables arranged with cloths and decorations (if possible)

☞ food and drinks for the "feasting"

☞ party blowers

☞ photocopies of the evaluation form found at the back of this session (and a manila envelope to collect them in)

☞ optional: a musician or a CD with familiar and favorite worship music

☞ optional: Prepare personal "party favors" for each woman: a ribbon or bracelet band for a simple bracelet with three alphabet beads—an S, a D, and a G. (Supplies available at craft stores.) You could use these as gifts, handing them out to the women after the teaching about Bach or at the end of the session.

❧ Preparing for This Session ❧

Two weeks before this session:

• Ask a team to decorate the room in a festive atmosphere.

• Assign each small group to bring food to the party.

• Ask every woman to be prepared to share some experience or "ah-ha" moment she has had with God over this 10-session study. (A time limit of three to four minutes per person is recommended for larger groups.)

- Gather photos that women have taken during the study. Prepare a slide show.

- Plan the time loosely. For the large group share time, you might want to pre-select the person who shares first and the person who shares last, ensuring you start and end with powerful stories and experiences. The rest of the women could share as they feel ready.

⁓ *Enrichment for Leaders* ⁓

Are you so busy planning ahead for your next responsibility that you never pause…and celebrate what God *has* done and *is* doing? The theme of this last session is to experience God's joy as a group while you celebrate together! Spend time the week before this last session praying for each individual woman who has been a part of *Rendezvous—Joy Ride*.

After the 10th session of *Joy Ride*, gather all of your leadership team (even if you're the only one on the team!) and do some celebrating—meet at a restaurant, meet at a park for a picnic, do something to say "Hip, hip, hooray!" And if you're the only one on the team, invite a friend to join you for a time of celebration…maybe she'll join you in leading the next *Rendezvous* study!

Field Note

At the end of our 10-week session, we took the leadership team to see a musical. It was a fun night out plus a great way to say "thank you" for all their hard work. We were able to pay for the evening with funds from the registration money.

1. Setting Up

As the women arrive, they will join their small group at a table.

Read together Philippians 4:20.

> "Always be full of joy in the Lord. I say it again—rejoice!"
> Philippians 4:4
>
> "Now all glory to God our Father forever and ever! Amen."
> Philippians 4:20

Slide 10.1

Say: **Notice the way Paul, the one who had every human reason to complain, closed out his letter to his dear friends.** (Read the verses again.) **For Paul, life truly was all about God!**

On every manuscript copy of Johann Sebastian Bach's musical compositions, you will find the letters SDG at the bottom. No, they aren't his initials. They stand for Soli Deo Gloria—Latin for "glory to God alone."

Who knows—maybe he learned that from Paul!

During our time together now, let's think in terms of SDG—Glory to God alone!

Read Philippians 4:4:

"Always be full of joy in the Lord. I say it again—rejoice!" **Let's take Paul's advice throughout his letter and use this session to really rejoice together!**

Take this opportunity to share with the women some of your own personal highlights and stories from the previous weeks. This is also a great time to say a public thank you to key leaders in the group. Make sure they get individually thanked for the specific work they have done.

Have every woman share at their tables an "ah-ha" they had with God during the 10-week session. Explain it can be something new they learned, an experience they had, a specific verse that impacted them, and so on. Allow at least 10 minutes for this.

2. Festivities

After the small group time, invite a few women to share with the large group: a part of her story, an experience, or an expression of her praise to God any way she chooses. Guide this part of the session by inserting your own words as necessary to encourage various women to share. You might need to remind them of a time limit if your group is large.

You may choose to have music, live or on CD, playing softly in the background. Arrange this as formally or as informally as you think is best for your group. It could be fun to have each woman who shares blow on her party blower before she begins talking. Then, after a woman finishes sharing, have everyone blow on their horns (at the same time) as a joyful noise, giving God the glory. You might want to have them share from their tables (use a wireless microphone if your group is larger than about 25 women), or you can invite them to come to the front.

Close this portion and transition into the feasting by leading the group in a time of prayer. You could do this in several ways: 1) Before the session you could ask a few women to be ready to pray before the feast. 2) You could give the women an opportunity to pray in their small groups. 3) You could pray as a large group, encouraging women to pray out loud from their seats.

3. Feasting

During the time of eating and visiting, project photos that have been taken throughout the study weeks. Background music is also a nice touch! Keep the photos replaying (as most women will enjoy seeing them more than once).

Field Note

We've done the party blower suggestion, and women loved it. It also helps women not be as nervous to share and creates a very festive atmosphere.

 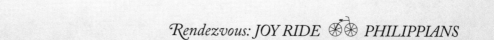

4. Evaluations

Encourage women to complete the evaluations and leave them in a marked manila envelope on their way out.

Thank You for Choosing *Rendezvous*!

We pray these last weeks have brought you and the women in your ministry to new highs of joy and intimacy in your relationship with God.
**For more great Bible studies and ministry resources,
visit www.group.com/women.**

Rendezvous—Joy Ride Evaluation

&❧ How did you hear about this study?

&❧ What was the biggest lesson you learned during this study?

&❧ Did this study help you find joy in God?

&❧ What was your favorite thing about this study?

&❧ Least favorite?

&❧ Would you be interested in doing another study?

If you'd like to hear about more upcoming studies, please give us your contact information.

Name:

Phone Number:

Address:

E-mail Address: